ST MATHEMATICS

4a

Collins Educational
An imprint of HarperCollins*Publishers*

Published 1994 by Collins Educational
77-85 Fulham Palace Road
London W6 8JB

An imprint of HarperCollins Publishers

© HarperCollins Publishers Ltd

Reprinted 1994, 1995

ISBN 0 00 313838–0

Series Editor: Anne Woodman
Co-Editor: Paul Harling
Consultant Editor: Eric Albany

Illustrations: Tim Archbold (pages 28, 98, 108, 112), Valerie Baines
    (page 105), Olivia Bown (pages 4, 78), Belinda Evans (page 12),
    Jean de Lemos (pages 2, 3, 5, 13, 19, 21, 24, 33, 37, 56, 57, 60,
    67, 69, 71, 77, 83, 84, 86, 87, 95, 98, 99, 101, 102), Jenny
    Mumford (pages 7, 8, 10, 11, 15, 17, 18, 26, 29, 32, 41, 54, 58,
    61, 72, 76, 80, 82, 96, 97, 100), Julia Osorno (pages 1, 88),
    Archie Plumb (pages 22, 38, 42, 93, 103), Amelia Rosato (pages
    16, 20, 22, 25, 27, 45, 50, 55, 85, 115, 116, 117), Polly Shields
    (pages 54, 103), Jane Taylor (pages 3, 30, 31, 52, 53, 114),
    Totem Graphics (page 6), Peter Tucker (computer graphics,
    pages 41, 60, 70, 71, 72, 75, 98, 99, 101, 102, 119, 120), Martin
    Ursell (pages 23, 39, 43, 121)

Photographs: all Martin Sookias, apart from Action Plus (pages 90,
    91), Barnaby's Picture Library (pages 52, 118), Image Bank
    (cover), Letraset (pages 46, 47, 62), Milepost 92½ (page 74),
    Rover Cars (page 52)

Equipment: We should like to thank NES Arnold for lending
    equipment for photographs and artists' reference.

Design and typesetting: Alex Tucker, PGT Design, Oxford

Printing: Scotprint, Musselburgh, Scotland

STEPS ■ ■ ■ ■ ■ ■ ■ ■ ■ ■ 4a
MATHEMATICS

Contents

■ ■ ■ ■ ■ ■ ■ ■ ■ ■ ■ ■ ■ ■

The coloured blocks at the top of a page show you that the work is mainly about:

■ number   ■ algebra   ■ shape and space   ■ handling data   ■ measurement

A box like this at the top of a page tells you what you will need. We expect that you will always have a ruler, pencil, eraser and colouring materials so they aren't shown in the boxes.

balance-scales, rice, plastic bag

Knock out!

This is a game for two players.

I AM THE FIRST PLAYER. I KEY IN A 4-DIGIT NUMBER BUT I MUSTN'T USE 0.

I TELL THE SECOND PLAYER WHICH DIGIT TO **KNOCK OUT** – THAT MEANS CHANGE IT TO 0.

KNOCK OUT THE 2!

NOW IT'S MY TURN. I SUBTRACT THE NUMBER WHICH WILL **KNOCK OUT** THE DIGIT.

I HAD TO SUBTRACT 200 TO **KNOCK OUT** THE 2.

WE GO ON DOING THIS TILL THE DISPLAY SHOWS 0.

Try it with a partner. Use different 4-digit numbers.
Take it in turns to be the first and second players.

CHALLENGE

PLAY IT AGAIN – BUT THIS TIME THE FIRST PLAYER CHOOSES TWO DIGITS WHICH HAVE TO BE KNOCKED OUT BY SUBTRACTION.

OK

Abacus numbers

4-spike abacus, 9 beads

You could work with a friend to do these.

Use a **4-spike** abacus and **5** beads for each number you make.

I've made 2300.

I'll record mine like this ...

1   Find and record answers to these.

a The **smallest** and **largest** numbers possible.

b Six **4-digit numbers** between 3000 and 4000.

c Six **even** 4-digit numbers between 1000 and 2500.

d Three **odd** 4-digit numbers between 2000 and 3000.

e Numbers made by putting beads on the **2 left-hand** spikes only.

f Numbers with a 4 in them **in ascending order**.

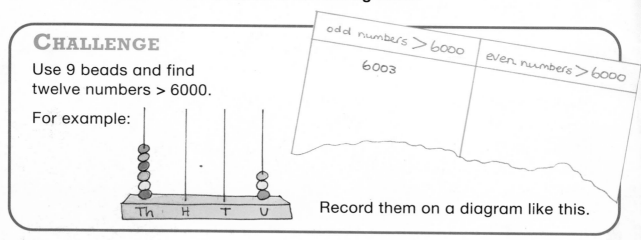

CHALLENGE

Use 9 beads and find twelve numbers > 6000.

For example:

odd numbers > 6000	even numbers > 6000
6003	

Record them on a diagram like this.

Place values

1 Write these numbers in words:

a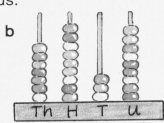

b

c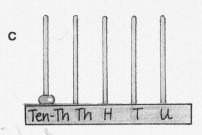

2 Write in figures:

a ten thousand

b eight thousand, one hundred

c seven thousand and four

d five thousand and thirty

e nine thousand

f seven hundred and two.

3 Copy. Write **>** or **<**, between each pair:

a 8254   8245   **b** 6004   6404   **c** 7101   7110.

4 Write a 4-digit number which has a:

a seven in the thousands column

b three in the ones column

c one in the tens column

d nine in the hundreds column.

5 Write the number which is 100 less than:

a 7000   **b** 5555   **c** 7111   **d** 9023   **e** 10 000.

6 Write the number which is 1000 more than:

a 9000   **b** 7888   **c** 6367   **d** 19   **e** 107.

CHALLENGE

You can make 24 different 4-digit numbers using these once each time:
True or false? Investigate.

Lines and angles

1 Decide whether the red lines on these objects are **parallel** or **perpendicular**.

a FRENCH

b shouties

c

d

e 10

f

g

h HAPPY BiRthdAY

i

j

2 Choose materials to draw and colour a pattern which has parallel **and** perpendicular lines.

Naming angles

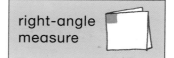
REMEMBER

Sharp angles **smaller** than
a right angle are called **acute** angles.

Blunt angles **larger** than
a right angle are called **obtuse** angles.

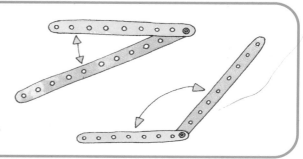

1 Use your right-angle measure to check whether the marked angles are **acute**, **obtuse** or **right angles**.
Write the answers in your book.

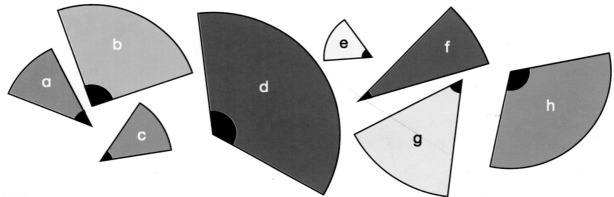

2 Decide what sort of angles these are.
Write your answers in your book.

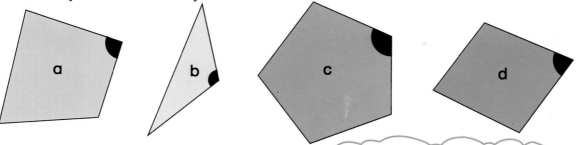

3 Use your ruler and right-angle measure to draw a shape which has:

a 3 sides and 1 **obtuse** angle
b 4 sides and 2 **acute** angles
c 5 sides and 1 **acute** angle
d 6 sides and 3 **acute** angles.

Keep trying if you don't get them right straight away.

Fishy multiples

You could work with a friend to try this.

1 Think of the best way you can to find and show the answers to these.

 a Answers in **both** the x 2 **and** the x 4 tables.

 b Answers in **both** the x 4 **and** x 8 tables.

 c Answers in **both** the x 2 **and** x 8 tables.

 d Answers in the x 2 **and** x 4 **and** x 8 tables.

Remember: if you multiply whole numbers together, the answer is a **multiple**.

CHALLENGE

Find and display in your own way numbers up to 80 which are **not** multiples of 2, 4 or 8.

Common multiples

1   Mark the numbers on the 100 square on RM 16 like this.

    a Put a ✕ over the multiples of 2.

    b Put a ◯ over the multiples of 4.

    c Put a ┼ over the multiples of 8.

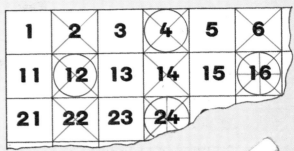

The numbers marked like this are multiples of 2 and 4.

2   In your book, describe the numbers marked like this:

    a   **b**   **c** ☐

3   Write the number which is the

    a 2nd multiple of 8   **b** 4th multiple of 4   **c** 8th multiple of 2

    d 3rd multiple of 8   **e** 6th multiple of 4   **f** 12th multiple of 2.

4   **a** List the numbers marked in this way:

    b Design a diagram like this for six of the numbers in **a**.

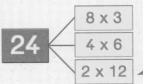

You could use a calculator to help you with this one!

5   Using only these numbers make as many x and ÷ sentences as you can.

2   8   64   4   16   32

Times in the day

1 Write 24-hour times for:

   a twenty to four in the afternoon
   b half past eight in the morning
   c a quarter to midnight
   d a quarter past five in the afternoon
   e five past four in the morning.

2 Write 12-hour times for:

   a 19:55
   b 13:05
   c 22:22
   d 17:45
   e 15:00.

REMEMBER

On the 24-hour clock,
8.00 pm is written as 20:00

You can find 24-hour times by adding 12 to pm times.

3 Sunita made a 24-hour timeline for one day:

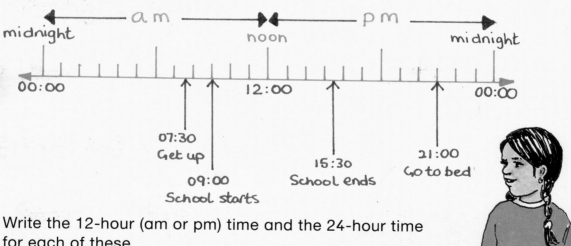

4 Write the 12-hour (am or pm) time and the 24-hour time for each of these.

   a Sunita's parents get up half an hour before she does.
   b Sunita has school dinner at midday.
   c She visits her grandparents an hour after school ends.
   d She watches TV starting two hours before bed-time.
   e She switches out the light after reading in bed for half an hour.

5 Make your own 24-hour timeline, showing times of what you do in one day. (Or use RM 20).

Setting a timer

Robin's family were going out for the evening. They wanted to record *Panorama*, *Neighbours*, *World in Action* and *Def II*. They had an empty 180-minute videotape.

1. List the programmes and the start and finish times Robin entered on the video.

2. Write how many spare minutes they had left on the tape.

3. • Choose the programmes your family or friends might want to record.
   • Repeat 1 and 2 .

Evening TV at a glance

Time	BBC1	BBC2	ITV	C4
5.30 / 17:30	5.35 Neighbours	5.30 One in Four	5.40 News	5.30 Cartoons
6.00 / 18:00	6.00 Six O' Clock news	6.00 Ryder Cup Golf	6.00 Home and Away	6.00 The Wonder Years
6.30 / 18:30	6.30 Midlands Today/ East Midlands Today	6.40 Def II: Band	6.25 Central News	6.30 The Henderson Kids
7.00 / 19:00	7.00 Wogan	7.10 Def II: Standing Room Only	7.00 The Krypton Factor	7.00 Channel 4 News
7.30 / 19:30	7.30 Watchdog	7.40 The Planned Miracle	7.30 Coronation Street	
8.00 / 20:00	8.00 Telly Addicts		8.00 Strike It Lucky	8.00 Brookside
8.30 / 20:30	8.30 Brush Strokes	8.30 FILM Ghost Dancing	8.30 World in Action	8.30 Inspector Morse
9.00 / 21:00	9.00 Nine O'Clock News		9.00 Champion-ship Boxing	
9.30 / 21:30	9.30 Panorama			
10.00 / 22:00			10.00 News at Ten	
	10.10			10.30

Addition trios

Jameela wanted to find the total of 6, 8 and 4.
She wrote down 6 + 4 + 8 = 18 because she
found this the easiest order to add the numbers.

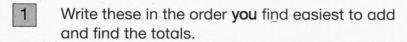

1 Write these in the order **you** find easiest to add
and find the totals.

    a 8, 7 and 2   **b** 9, 9 and 1   **c** 7, 5 and 5

    d 6, 2 and 8   **e** 4, 7 and 7   **f** 3, 8 and 4

2 Copy and complete these by finding the missing numbers.

    a 4 + 7 + 6 = ●   **b** ● + 9 + 3 = 13   **c** 6 + ● + 7 = 17

    d 9 + 8 + 1 = ●   **e** 8 + ● + 4 = 20   **f** ● + 5 + 7 = 19

    g 4 + ● + 6 = 17   **h** 9 + ● + 6 = 15   **i** ● + 3 + 9 = 20

On this addition wheel,
the three numbers on the spokes
total the number inside.

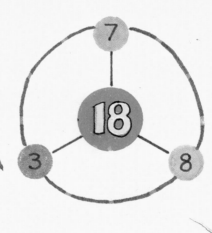

3 Design addition wheels, each with **18** inside, using these rules.

    a Three different even 1-digit numbers on the spokes.
    b Two odd and one even 1-digit numbers on the spokes.
    c The same number on every spoke.
    d The number on each spoke can be divided exactly by 3.
    e The number on each spoke is a different multiple of 2.
    f One 2-digit number and two 1-digit numbers on the spokes.

4 Here are the bits to make four different addition wheels.
Decide how to fit the wheels together and draw them.

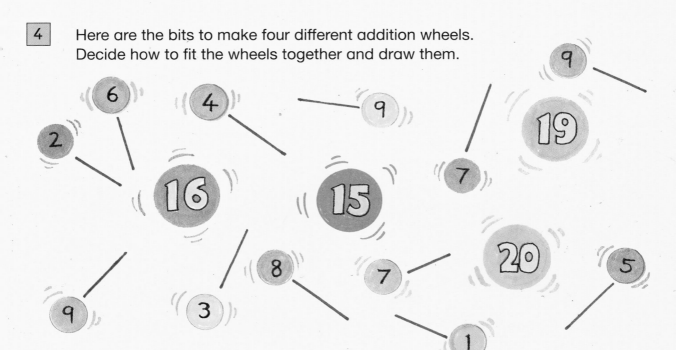

Try to find the answers to 5 in your head.

5 Work out the change from £20
if you buy these:

a felt tips and computer game
b cassette and teddy bear
c computer game and cassette
d tennis set and teddy bear
e magic kit and tennis set
f teddy bear and computer game
g computer game and magic kit.

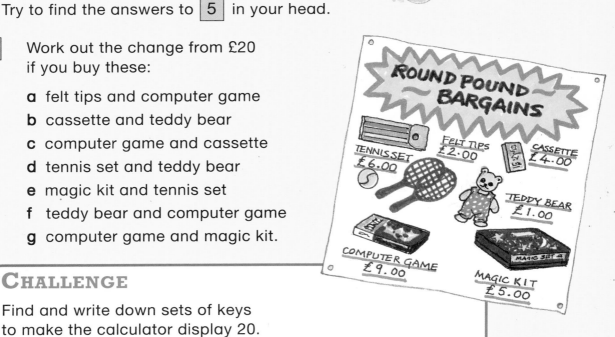

ROUND POUND BARGAINS

TENNIS SET £6.00
FELT TIPS £2.00
CASSETTE £4.00
TEDDY BEAR £1.00
COMPUTER GAME £9.00
MAGIC KIT £5.00

CHALLENGE

Find and write down sets of keys
to make the calculator display 20.

20.

Addition problems

1 Work out the answers **without** materials to help you.

a 63 children are in the school hall.
8 more children join them.
**How many children are
in the school hall altogether?**

b Martin is 89 cm tall.
Anna is 7 cm taller.
How tall is Anna?

2 Copy and continue these patterns until you reach £98.

a £8 ⌣+£9⌝ £17 ⌣+£9⌝ £26 +£9⌝ ...

b £7 ⌣+£7⌝ £14 +£7⌝ £21 + £7⌝ ...

c £38 +£6⌝ £44 +£6⌝ ...

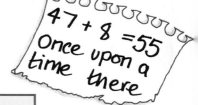

47 + 8 = 55
Once upon a
time there

3 Write a story to show what this might mean: 47 + 8 = 55

CHALLENGE

Use

Fit them in this frame:
You can make 24 different totals.
Try to find them all.

Bar-line graphs

RM 26 or 27

Gordon collected data about the numbers of letters
in people's last names.

He made a tally chart ...   ... and then drew a bar-line graph.

Numbers of letters	Tally	Total
2	I	1
3	II	2
4	ШШ ШШ	10
5	ШШ ШШ ШШ ШШ	20
6	ШШ ШШ ШШ ШШ IIII	24
7	ШШ ШШ II	12
8	ШШ	5
9	ШШ	5
10	II	2
more than 10	II	2

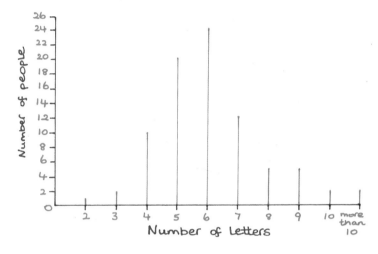

1   What was the most common length
    of name?

2   How many people had names
    with eight letters?

You could use class registers,
or the telephone book,
or lists of football teams.

3   Use RM 26 or RM 27 to make a tally
    chart and a bar-line graph to show
    the number of letters in the last name
    of about 80 people. Choose a scale
    for your bar-line graph.

4   Write six facts about your graph.
    Ask someone to check your facts.

CHALLENGE

Choose a topic to collect data on.
Draw a tally chart and a bar-line graph to show your results.

More bar-line graphs! ■ ■ ■ ■

Helen and Raju were rolling dice
and recording their score.

They drew a bar-line graph
to show their results.

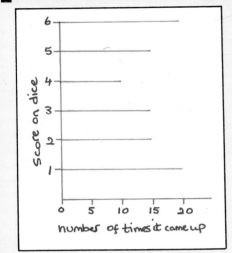

1   **a** How many times was
the dice rolled altogether?

   b How many times was
an even number scored?

2   Year 5 has been collecting stickers.

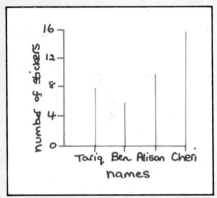

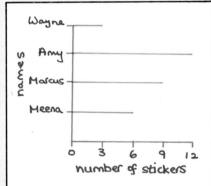

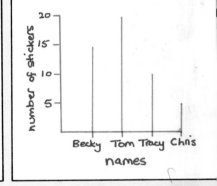

a Who collected the most stickers?

b Which two pairs of children collected
the same number of stickers?

c Who collected the smallest
number of stickers?

d Write a list of the names and numbers
of stickers in order from largest to smallest.

CHALLENGE

Collect and record data about friends' favourite sports.
Draw two different bar-line graphs to show the results.
Use a different scale for each graph.

Take-away pencils

Find the answers in your own way. Write down anything that helps.

1 Pairs of children took some pencils from pots holding 20 pencils. Work out how many pencils will be **left in the pot** each time. Write the answers in your book.

a I've removed seven.

So have I.

b I've removed two more than nine.

I've taken out two less than nine.

d I've taken five.

c I've taken nine.

I've got six.

I've taken eight.

2 Work out the answers to these.

a 14 − 3 − 5 =   **b** 17 − 7 − 4 =   **c** 19 − 5 − 2 =
d 12 − 3 − 9 =   **e** 18 − 4 − 4 =   **f** 20 − 6 − 7 =

3 Find the missing numbers.

a 10 − 3 − ☐ = 2   **b** 14 − ☐ − 3 = 9   **c** ☐ − 4 − 4 = 9
d 13 − 2 − ☐ = 6   **e** 15 − ☐ − 5 = 0   **f** 16 − ☐ − 6 = 6
g 14 − 7 − ☐ = 1   **h** ☐ − 2 − 8 = 5   **i** 20 − ☐ − 8 = 4

4 Write a story for this subtraction: 14 − 4 − 7 = 3.

CHALLENGE

Continue this pattern as far as you can.

20	−		−		=2
19	−		−		=2
18	−		−		=2
17	−		−		=2

Patterns and problems

1 Copy and complete these patterns.

a 68, 66, 64, 62, ☐, ☐, ☐ . **b** 47, 42, 37, ☐, ☐, ☐ .

c ☐, ☐, ☐, 68, 58, 48. **d** 54, 47, ☐, ☐, ☐, 19.

e 81, 72, ☐, ☐, ☐ . **f** 77, ☐, ☐, ☐, 57, 52.

2 Write the number 6 less than each of these.

  a 17 **b** 38 **c** 54 **d** 61 **e** 80

3 Try to work out the missing numbers in your head.
Then copy and complete the **blue** sentences.

  a Ajit's bike costs £82. Paul's bike costs £7 less.
  Paul's bike costs £_____ .

  b Emma is 8 cm shorter than Ricky. Ricky is 95 cm tall.
  Emma is _____ cm tall.

  c Carla's dad weighed 85 kg. He lost 9 kg in weight on his diet.
  Carla's dad now weighs _____ kg.

CHALLENGE

If 74 + 5 = 79, then 79 − 5 = 74.
Make up more sentences like this using these numbers.

45   52   7   10   42   34   8   38

Triangle angles

1 cm squared paper
or use RMA

You can use
squared paper
to draw right angles.

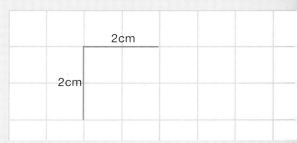

2cm

2cm

1 Draw right angles on squared paper to match these.

a
2cm
3cm

b
4cm
3cm

c
2cm
6cm

f
8cm
4cm

d
1cm
5cm

e
1cm
1cm

2 Measure and then draw these in the same way.

a   b   c   d

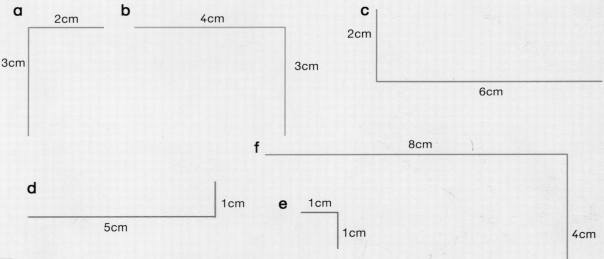

3 Add one line to change each right angle into
a **right-angled triangle**.

4 Beside each triangle, write **isosceles** or **scalene**.

REMEMBER

An isosceles triangle has two sides of the same length.

A scalene triangle has no sides of the same length.

More triangle angles

Jo numbered the corners of a paper triangle and tore it into three pieces.

Then she drew a straight line.

She found that the corners fitted together on the line.

She glued them down to show her teacher.

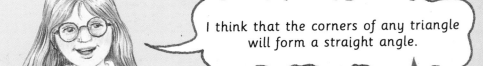

I think that the corners of any triangle will form a straight angle.

1 Experiment with different triangles to find out if what Jo thinks is true.

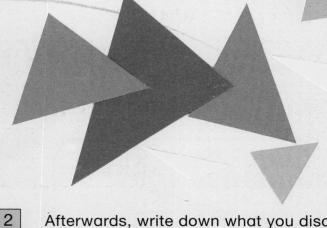

2 Afterwards, write down what you discover.

Seeing percentages

> **Per cent** means 'out of a hundred'.
> The symbol for per cent is **%**.
> If 20 parts out of 100 are coloured
> it is written as **20% coloured**.

1 For each shape, write the percentage coloured green

a 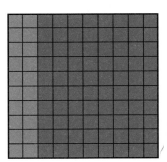   b 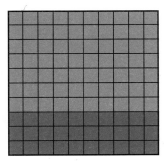   c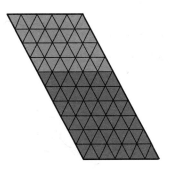

2 For each shape in **1**, write the percentage coloured **purple**

3 Colour the grids on RM 36 like this:

a **Grid 1**	b **Grid 2**	c **Grid 3**	d **Grid 4**
10% orange	20% red	50% orange	70% blue
30% blue	40% green	50% purple	10% red

4 Underneath each grid on RM 36, write the percentage **not** coloured.

5 For each of these shapes, write the percentage which is blue.

a 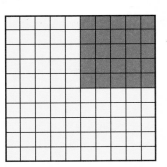   b 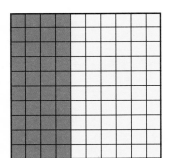   c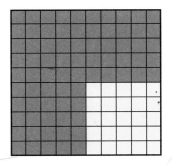

6 Now write each amount coloured blue as a fraction.

...and more percentages

RM 36, glue pen, scissors

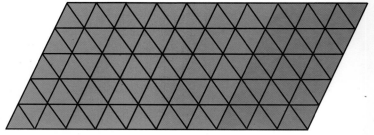

On this grid of 100 triangles
40% are green
30% are red
30% are blue.

1 **a** Colour the grids on RM 36 to create patterns.
   b Cut out each pattern and glue it in your book.
   c Underneath each one, write the percentages of colours used.

2 **a** Draw a square.
      Colour 100% of it.

   b Draw a circle.
      Colour 0% of it.

3 Copy these shapes. Write percentages in the circles
   to make each side add up to 100%.

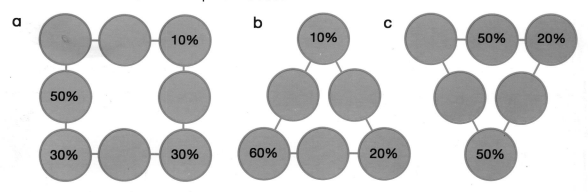

a

10%

50%

30%   30%

b

10%

60%   20%

c

50%   20%

50%

4 Something is wrong with these statements.
   Write about them.

b 150% of my friends like to eat ice cream.

c Our rounders team won 50% of its games, lost 30% of them, so we drew 30% of the games.

a In my class 50% of the children are boys and 40% of the children are girls.

Zig-zags

This line is $5\frac{1}{2}$ cm or 5·5 cm long.

1 Draw lines of these lengths.

    a 9·5 cm   **b** 11·5 cm   **c** 3·5 cm   **d** 0·5 cm

    e 2 cm longer than 8·5 cm   **f** 3 cm shorter than 16·5 cm

    g half as long as 13 cm   **h** three times as long as 2·5 cm

---

These zig-zags each measure 10 cm in length.

a

6·5 cm

3·5 cm

5·5 cm

b

2 cm

2·5 cm

6·5 cm + 3·5 cm = 10 cm   5·5 cm + 2 cm + 2·5 cm = 10 cm

---

2 Draw 5 different 10 cm zig-zags like example **a**.

3 Draw 5 different 10 cm zig-zags like example **b**.

4 Try to swap your zig-zags with a friend and check each other's work.

CHALLENGE

- Draw the longest zig-zag you can with lengths which include half cm lengths.

- Find its total length.

Mainly millimetres

1 Draw lines of these lengths.

    a 44 mm   **b** 27 mm   **c** 61 mm

    d 86 mm   **e** 52 mm   **f** 17 mm

    g 30 mm   **h** 93 mm   **i** 75 mm

REMEMBER
Use a very sharp pencil and measure from the zero mark on your ruler.

2 Measure these strips in millimetres and then draw lines of the same length. Underneath, write the lengths in different ways.

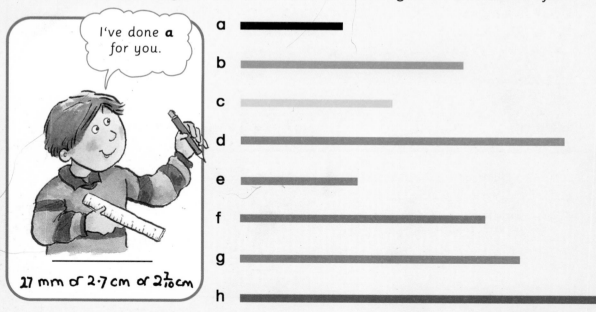

I've done **a** for you.

27 mm or 2·7 cm or 2 7/10 cm

a
b
c
d
e
f
g
h

CHALLENGE

62 mm

38 mm

Design more 100 mm zig-zags like this one.

Car distances

1 Find the distance in kilometres between these villages.

a Ambred and Moleshill
b Elmbridge and Ambred
c Ambred and Pondbury
d Pondbury and Oakwood

e Moleshill and Oakwood via Bramblewood
f Elmbridge and Firtop via Greenton
g Firtop and Bramblewood via Greenton
h Greenton and Bramblewood

2 Kate lives in Ambred and is going to visit her Gran in Oakwood.
She is going via Pondbury to collect her cousin Paul.
When she has travelled these distances,
which two villages will she be between?

a 8 km   **b** 21 km   **c** 30 km

d 45 km   **e** 27 km   **f** 15 km

> We've travelled 12 km and we're between Greenton and Moleshill.

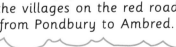

3 Copy and complete this signpost.

> This signpost shows all the villages on the red road from Pondbury to Ambred.

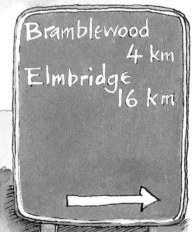

> Bramblewood 4 km
> Elmbridge 16 km

CHALLENGE

Design a map of your own like the one on this page.
Write questions to ask about it.

Mental addition

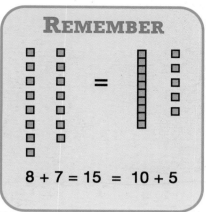

8 + 7 = 15 = 10 + 5

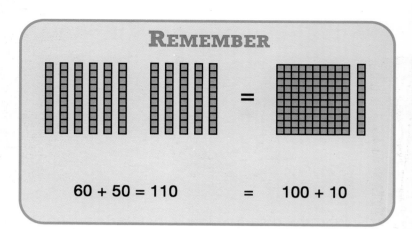

60 + 50 = 110 = 100 + 10

1 Write these in the same way.

a 7 + 7 =   b 9 + 6 =
c 9 + 4 =   d 5 + 8 =
e 8 + 8 =   f 9 + 8 =

2 Now write these.

a 60 + 70 =   b 90 + 80 =
c 50 + 60 =   d 50 + 70 =
e 90 + 20 =   f 80 + 50 =

This number balance shows
the same information.

This number balance shows
the same information.

3 Design 2 number balances
for each of these.

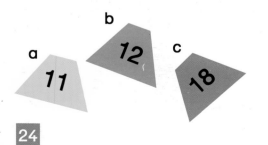

a 11
b 12
c 18

4 Design 2 number balances
for each of these.

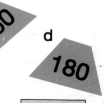

a 140
b 150
c 160
d 180

Number neighbours

These empty seats show examples of number neighbours.

1 Find totals up to 20 by adding number neighbours.

We've done one for you.

$$2 + 3 + 4 = 9$$

Use a calculator to help you if you want.

CHALLENGE

1 2 3 4 5 6 7 8 9 **10**

- By adding number neighbours together, you can make 20 totals which are even numbers.

- Find as many of these as you can.

Setting out sums

Callum and Azara have favourite ways of adding.

I like this way.

```
   146
 +581
     7   (6 + 1)
   120   (40 + 80)
   600   (100 + 500)
   727
```

I like this way.

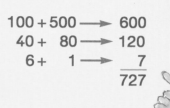

```
100 + 500 ──▶ 600
 40 +  80 ──▶ 120
  6 +   1 ──▶   7
              727
```

1   Find the sum of these in **your** favourite way.

   a 256 + 550   **b** 453 + 339   **c** 780 + 125

   d 328 + 345   **e** 169 + 772   **f** 608 + 259

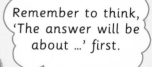

Remember to think, 'The answer will be about ...' first.

2   Use addition to find the numbers which are double these.

   a 437   **b** 166   **c** 396
   d 275   **e** 358   **f** 409

CHALLENGE

It is impossible to make more than ten different totals by adding pairs of these numbers together.

134   247
   475
        514
326

True or false? Decide how to find out if Lucy is correct.

Skittle addition

calculator

Rachel, Gopal and Rory made a skittle game.

The player knocking over the skittles with the highest total in each game won.

This table shows the skittles they knocked over in 3 games.

	Game 1			Game 2			Game 3			
Rachel	156	241	5	325		67	325		370	
Gopal	325		67	241	370	5	5	67	43	156
Rory	67	370	43	43		156	67	43	241	

1 **a** Work out the total scored in game 1 by

  ■ Rachel ■ Gopal ■ Rory

  b Write who won game 1.

2 Work out who won game 2 in the same way.

3 Copy and complete these sentences about game 3.

  a _____ won with a score of _____ .
  b _____ had the smallest score with _____ .
  c _____ and _____ scored between 200 and 400.
  d Rory scored ____ which was ____ points more than Gopal.

CHALLENGE

My highest score ever with 3 skittles was 762.

My lowest score ever with 3 skittles was 266.

Work out which skittles gave these scores.

Calculator display ■ ■ ■

Peter and Kate had to work out how to reverse 142 to 241 on their calculator display.

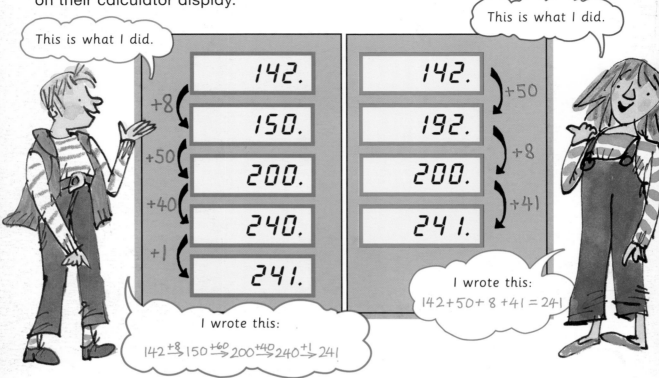

This is what I did.

This is what I did.

I wrote this:
$142 \xrightarrow{+8} 150 \xrightarrow{+60} 200 \xrightarrow{+40} 240 \xrightarrow{+1} 241$

I wrote this:
$142 + 50 + 8 + 41 = 241$

1. Reverse these numbers, using as few additions as you can. Record in your own way.

a **263.**   b **182.**   c **306.**   d **415.**

e **217.**   f **466.**   g **345.**   h **569.**

CHALLENGE

One answer is
$451 + 326 = 777$

Using these keys once each, find different odd totals between 700 and 900.

1 2 3 4 5 6 + =

28

Nesting cubes ■ ■ ■

1 cm squared paper or RMA,
scissors, card, glue

Try to work with a partner.

1   Decide how to make 3 cubes which fit inside each other.

2   Choose how to make the nets.

It helps if you score the folds
and decorate the boxes before
you glue them.

We'll have to make sure
the lids on the medium
and large cubes open.

Finding nets

These 6 tiles are a net because they fold up to make this special hexahedron.

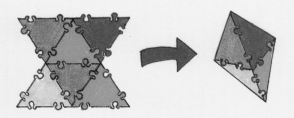

A **hexahedron** is **any** 3-D shape with 6 flat faces

Some of these shapes are nets.
Which ones, do you think?

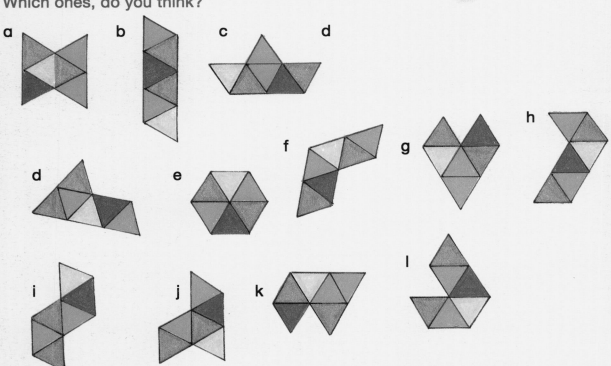

a b c d

d e f g h

i j k l

✓ means 'is a net'
✗ means 'is not a net'

a	✓
b	
c	

1 Make and fold up each shape to find out which are nets.

Keep a record.

STEPS 4a:12

2   Make a sorting diagram like this on RM D.

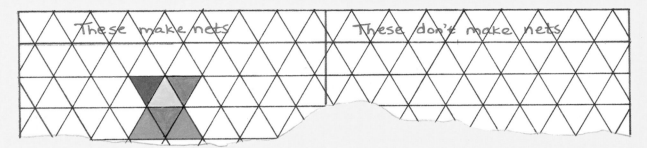

REVISION FACES, EDGES AND VERTICES

1   Find examples of these.

a cube

b square-based pyramid

c cylinder

d hexagonal prism

e cuboid

f cone

g triangular prism

h tetrahedron

2   Copy and complete this table for each of the shapes.

	3-D shapes	faces	edges	vertices
a	cube	6	12	8

Cuboid nets

cuboids, 1 cm squared paper or RMA, scissors

Work with others if you can.

Nicola, Steven, Clare and Salim each tried to design a net for a cuboid.
When they folded the nets up, only three of them made a cuboid.
Here are the four designs.

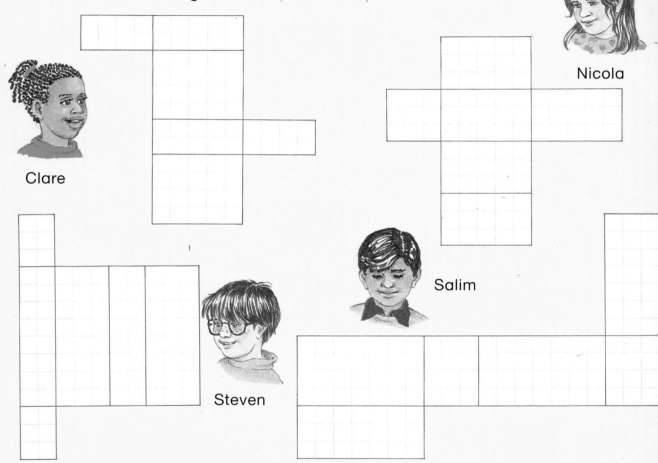

Clare

Nicola

Salim

Steven

1   Together, decide whose net will **not** make a cuboid.

2   Make the four nets to see if you are correct.

CHALLENGE

Remake the net which will not make a cuboid so that it works.
Change it as little as possible.

Counting on and back

Playing a dice game, Tanya scored 145 and Jack scored 221.

They wanted to work out the difference.

Tanya counted on like this:

$$145 \xrightarrow{+5} 150 \xrightarrow{+50} 200 \xrightarrow{+20} 20 \xrightarrow{+1} 1$$

Difference = 76

Jack counted back like this.

$$221 \xrightarrow{-21} 200 \xrightarrow{-50} 150 \xrightarrow{-5} 145$$

$$221 \xrightarrow{-76} 145$$

1   Count on like Tanya to find the difference between these scores. Use as few arrows as you can.

     a 365 and 440   **b** 150 and 235   **c** 237 and 320
     d 115 and 209   **e** 456 and 543   **f** 609 and 697

2   Count back like Jack to check your answers for **1** .

3   Copy and complete this table.

This shows the score when we played a game six times.

Scores	Tanya	Jack	difference
Game 1	234	326	
2	550	475	
3	190	278	
4	185	241	
5	479	404	
6	223	310	

4   The player with the larger total in the difference column wins.
Who won? Show how you found out.

Calculator subtraction

Use only the arrowed keys
on your calculator.

1 **a** Choose digits to go here. ☐ ☐ ☐ ☐ ☐ ☐ ☐

    b Make the calculator display as many different answers as you can.

    c Record each subtraction.

> Here's one example:
> 312 − 45 = 267

2 Write headings like these
and put your subtractions under each heading.

a Answers from 0 to 99

b Answers from 100 to 199

c Answers from 200 to 299

d Answers from 300 to 399

e Answers from 400 to 499

f Answers from 500 to 599

3 Compare results with your friends.

Co-ordinate points

1 Read the co-ordinates to find and write the names of 5 cities.

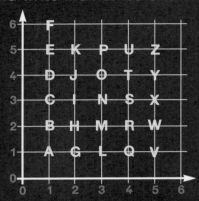

REMEMBER

The horizontal axis comes first when you read or write co-ordinates.

a (5,4) (3,4) (4,2) (2,5)
b (1,4) (3,4) (5,1) (1,5) (4,2)
c (2,1) (3,1) (1,1) (4,3) (2,1) (3,4) (5,2)
d (1,3) (1,1) (4,2) (1,4) (2,3) (1,6) (1,6)
e (3,1) (3,4) (3,3) (1,4) (3,4) (3,3)

2 Use the co-ordinates code from **1** to write:

a the name of the place where you live   **b** your first name.

3

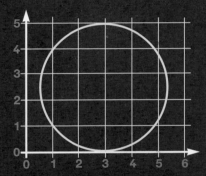

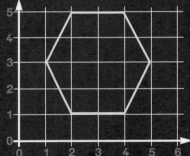

Write the co-ordinates of:

a 4 points on the **rim** of a circle
b 2 points **outside** the circle
c 3 points **inside** the circle

d 4 points **inside** the hexagon
e 2 points **outside** the hexagon
f 3 **corners** of the hexagon.

CHALLENGE

- Use RM 60 or draw your own grids.
- On each grid draw a different square with its centre at point (3,3).
- Write the co-ordinates for the corners.

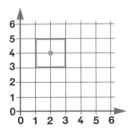

This square's centre is at point (2,4).

Next-door four

2 dice numbered 1-6,
(white, coloured),
small counters, RM 59

The white dice will tell you the **first** number of the co-ordinates.
(The number to move **across** the grid. ➡)

The coloured dice will tell you the second number of the co-ordinates.
(The number to move **up** the grid. ⬆)

This throw gives you (1,3)

1   Roll both dice.

- The score tells you the co-ordinates of a point.
- Put a counter on that point on RM 59.
- Keep rolling and placing counters
  until you have four counters in a row
  and four counters in a column.

2   Record the co-ordinates of the four counters in order

   a from **left to right**   **b** from **bottom to top**.

3   Write a sentence about each pattern of numbers.

Making shapes ■ ■ ■ ■ ■

HELP BOX

On this grid, these points were marked.
(3,3) (6,3) (6,1) (3,1)

The points were joined **in order**
with straight lines.
(3,3) → (6,3) → (6,1) → (3,1) → (3,3)

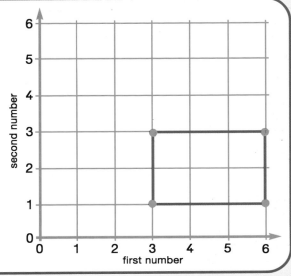

1   On RM 60, mark these points then join them **in order**.
(Use a different grid for each group.)

a (4,6) (6,2) (2,2) (4,6)
b (2,6) (2,0) (6,0) (2,6)
c (0,5) (6,4) (2,1) (0,5)
d (3,1) (1,3) (3,5) (5,3) (3,1)
e (5,3) (5,5) (2,6) (0,4) (2,2) (5,3)

I'm a hexagon!

2   On RM 60, grid **f**, mark 6 points.
Join them in order to construct a hexagon.
Write the order in which you joined the points.

You went wrong there.

CHALLENGE

- Draw your own grid on squared paper.
- Draw a picture or shape with straight lines.
- List the co-ordinates in order on a separate sheet.
- Challenge a friend to draw your picture
  using the list of co-ordinates only.
- Afterwards, compare your pictures.

Square centimetres

This square has an area of one square centimetre, also written as 1 sq cm.

area coloured = 1 sq cm

 or

area coloured = $\frac{1}{2}$ sq cm

 or

area coloured = $\frac{1}{4}$ sq cm

1 Work out the area of each of these shapes.

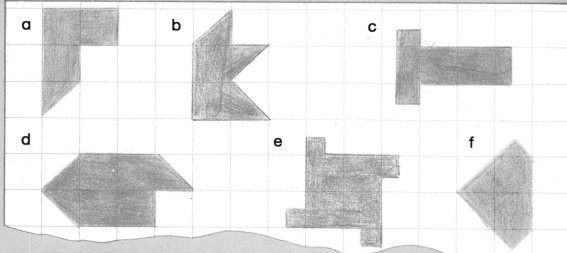

a   b   c

d   e   f

2 These shapes have an area of 4 square centimetres.

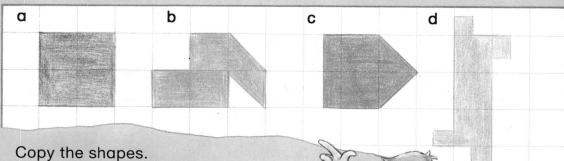

a   b   c   d

Copy the shapes.
Then draw more with an area of 4 sq cm.

Try to include $\frac{1}{2}$ or $\frac{1}{4}$ squares in each shape.

Area and perimeter

I've shown the areas. You write the perimeters.

1   Copy and complete these torn rectangles.

a

b

30 sq cm

c

22 sq cm

d

28 sq cm

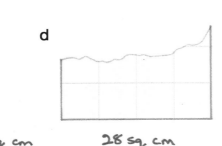

e

27 sq cm

area = 18 sq cm

2   **a**   Complete this torn rectangle in 3 different ways.

      b   Then find the perimeters of your 3 rectangles.

24 sq cm

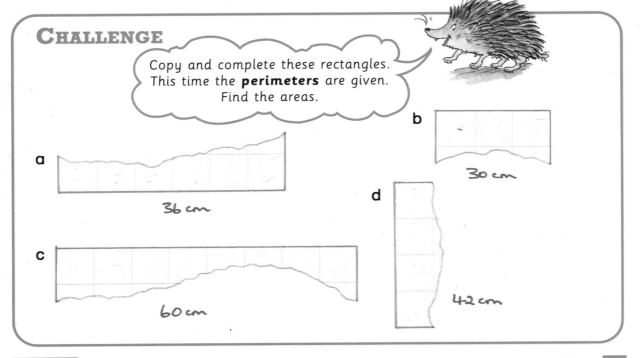

CHALLENGE

Copy and complete these rectangles. This time the **perimeters** are given. Find the areas.

a

36 cm

b

30 cm

c

60 cm

d

42 cm

Hexominoes

interlocking square tiles, RMA or 1 cm squared paper

These are hexominoes.

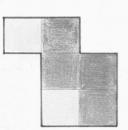 

These are **not** hexominoes.

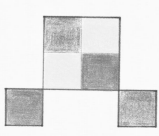 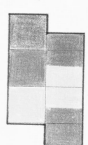

These hexominoes have the same area **and** perimeter.

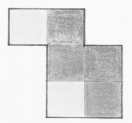

area = 6 sq cm
perimeter = 12 cm

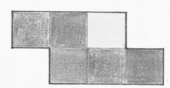

area = 6 sq cm
perimeter = 12 cm

1 Hexominoes all have the same area, but can they have different perimeters?
Use squared paper to find out.

Try to make sure your hexominoes are different.
Not like these.

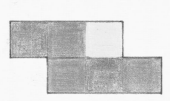  

It's the same shape turned round!

Interlocking tiles might help you.

2 Write about what you find out.

 STEPS 4a:15

Rod surfaces

Gary is estimating the total area of Cuisenaire rods.
He checks his estimates by drawing nets of the rods
on 1 cm squared paper.
This is what he wrote for the green rod.

Estimated area = 14 sq cm
Actual area = 14 sq cm

Remember to estimate first.

1 Choose one rod at a time
and do the same as Gary.

2 List the rods in ascending order
of their areas.
Your list might start like this.

Total area

white rod   6 sq cm
red rod

3 Write about any patterns you have found.

CHALLENGE

Investigate the total length of the **edges**
of each rod. Show what you do to find out.
Write about any patterns you find.

Reading scales

1 Write the weights shown on these scales.

a

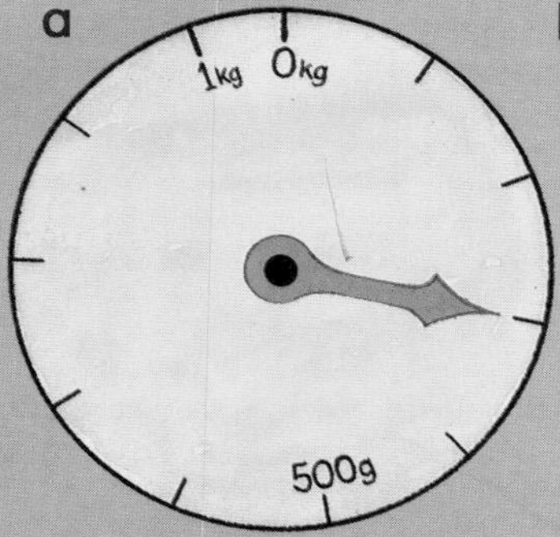

b

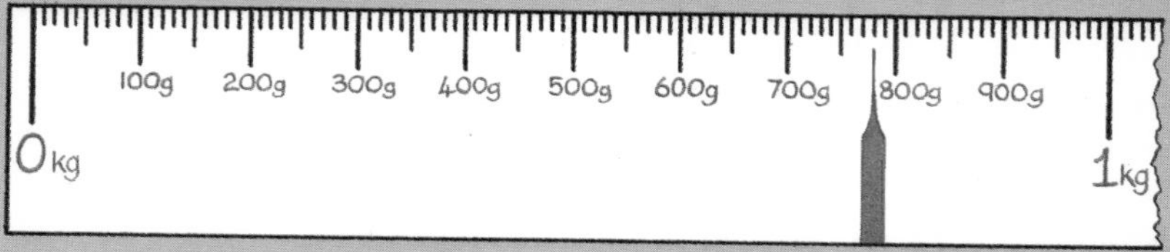

c

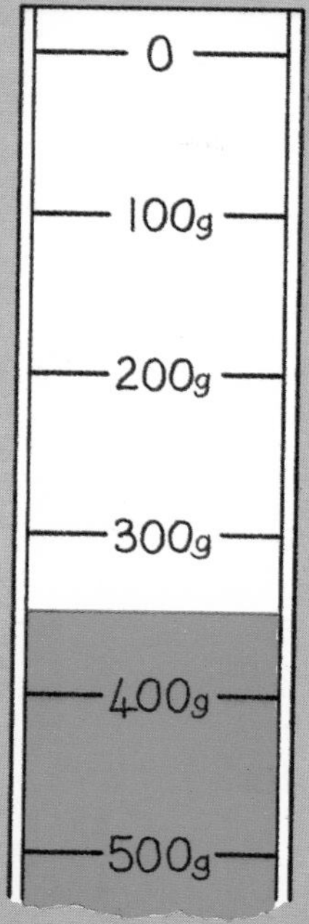

d

e

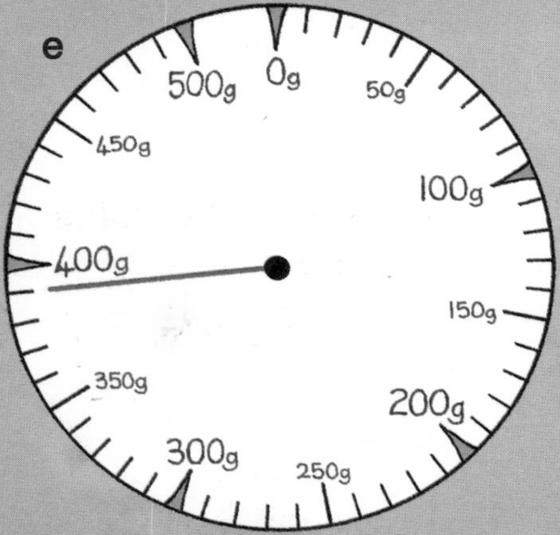

f

g

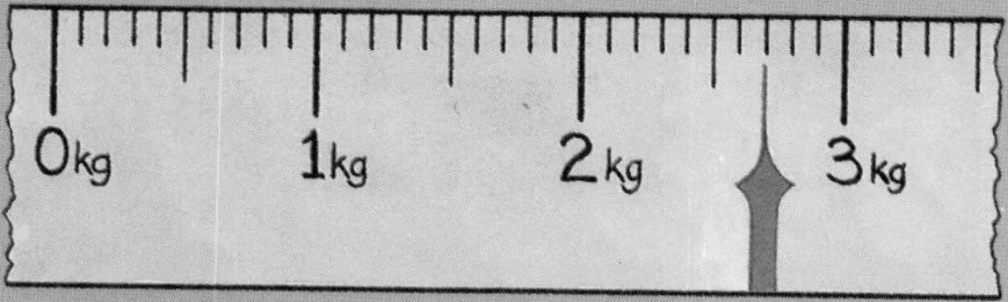

h

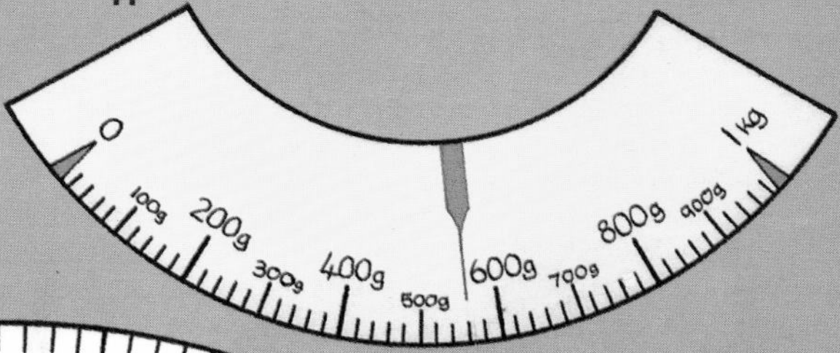

i

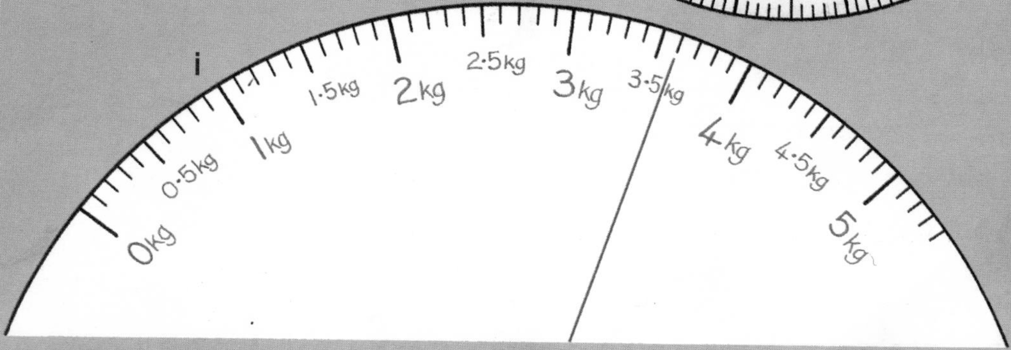

42

STEPS 4a:16

Grams and kilograms

1 Write these weights in **grams**.

Like this!
2kg 150g = 2000g + 150g = 2150g

 a 4 kg 900 g   b 1 kg 330 g
 c 2 kg 70 g   d 1 kg 55 g
 e 3 kg 8 g   f 5 kg 5 g

2 Write these weights in **kilograms** and **grams**.

Like this!
1200g = 1000g + 200g = 1kg 200g

 a 2370 g   b 1895 g
 c 4720 g   d 1001 g

1g   5g   10g   20g   50g   100g   200g   500g   1kg

3 Choose 3 standard weights to balance these totals.

 a 270 g   b 560 g

4 Choose 4 standard weights to balance these totals.

 a 1710 g   b 370 g

5 Would you use grams (g) or kilograms (kg) to weigh these objects?

a
matches

b
computer

c
sponge

d
coal

e
person

f
mouse

g
candy floss

h
large hammer

6 Write these weights in order, lightest first.

a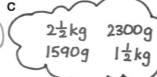

 a 1400g   1½kg   750g   2kg

 b 540g   450g   1½kg   600g

 c 2½kg   2300g   1590g   1½kg

Weighty problems

balance scales, 50g and 200g weights, Plasticene

600 g

2 kg

350 g

1 kg

420 g

150 g

1 Work out the weight of the food from each basket.

a   b   c   d

2 How much heavier is the bag of rice than the cabbage?

3 There are 10 biscuits in the packet. What does each one weigh?

4 A box of cereal holds 10 servings. Work out the weight of each serving.

CHALLENGES

- A cat and its kitten have a total weight of 3 kg.
  The cat weighs 2000 g more than the kitten. **What does the kitten weigh?**

- Use only balance scales, a 50 g weight, a 200 g weight and Plasticene.
  Write about ways to make lumps of Plasticene which weigh:
  a 250 g   **b** 150 g   **c** 100 g   **d** 50 g   **e** 25 g.

STEPS 4a:16

2-place decimals

RM A, RM 68, glue pen, calculator

1. Cut out a 10 x 10 grid from the squared paper.

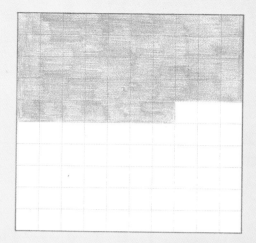

2. **a** Colour some of the squares.
  b Glue the grid in your book.
  c Underneath, write the fraction coloured and the fraction not coloured as **2-place decimal numbers**.
  d On your calculator, add these together to make sure they total 1.
  e Record the sum underneath.

Here's one of mine.

0·47 coloured
0·53 not coloured
0·47 + 0·53 = 1

3. Repeat **1** and **2** two more times.

4. Design and write about a symmetrical pattern like this: ⟶

Use one, two or three colours. I've used red and green and white.

0·24 green
0·32 red
0·44 white
0·24 + 0·32 + 0·44 = 1

5. Design another pattern with 2 lines of symmetry so that 0·08 is yellow and 0·56 blue.

6. **a** Use the grids on RM 68.
  b Colour squares on pairs of grids.
  c Use > or < to compare them.
  d Glue them in your book.

 >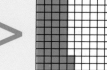

0·79 > 0·42

More 2-place decimals

£1·75
- 5 hundredths ──→ 5p
- 7 tenths ──→ 70p
- 1 whole ──→ £1

Write these amounts in the same way.

a £2·22   **b** £0·10   **c** £1·01

2 Write 6 amounts of money between £5 and £10 in the same way.

3 Write the decimals that complete these:

a 127p is the same as £ [•]

b 60p is the same as £ [•]   **c** 5p is the same as £ [•]

d 222 cm is the same as [•] m   **e** 50 cm is the same as [•] m

f 3 m and 26 cm is the same as [•] m.

4

1 whole   3 tenths   7 hundredths ──→ 1·37

Write these amounts as 2-place decimals:

a 2 wholes, 5 tenths and 1 hundredth   **b** 9 tenths and 7 hundredths
c 1 whole and 2 tenths   **d** 2 wholes and 6 hundredths
e 4 hundredths   **f** 8 tenths.

5 Write the next three numbers in each sequence.

a 0·37   0·38   0·39   ____   ____   ____
b 0·83   0·81   0·79   ____   ____   ____
c 0·25   0·31   0·37   ____   ____   ____
d 0·96   0·97   0·98   ____   ____   ____

6 Write a 2-place decimal that is between the two numbers.

    a 0·6 and 0.7   **b** 1·1 and 1.0   **c** 2·2 and 2·3
    d 3·1 and 2.9   **e** 7·7 and 7.73   **f** 3·85 and 3·80

7 Write these amounts as decimals.

    a two point one four   **b** nought point seven seven
    c three point nought five   **d** five tenths
    e fifty hundredths   **f** one hundred hundredths

8 **a** Use these numerals once each time
      with the decimal point, to make ⟶
      6 different 2-place decimal numbers.

      3   **5**   **8**   **•**

   b Put the numerals into this frame
      in as many ways as you can
      to make the statement true. ⟶

9

 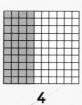

      1 • **4**   **9**

1·49 has 100 hundredths
+   40 hundredths
+   9 hundredths
_____
149 hundredths

How many hundredths altogether in these decimals?

   a 1·00   **b** 0·85   **c** 0·10   **d** 0·07   **e** 1·41   **f** 1·05

Building cuboids

interlocking centimetre cubes, RMA or 1 cm squared paper

This cuboid uses 16 centimetre cubes.

REMEMBER

Volume is the **amount of space** an object takes up.

- Its height is 2 cm. • Its length is 4 cm. • Its width is 2 cm.
- Its volume is 16 cubic centimetres.
- 16 cubic centimetres can be written 16 cu cm.

1 **a** Make as many different cuboids as you can with volumes of 16 cubic centimetres.

   b Record the height, length and width of each one.

2 **a** Draw this shape on squared paper. Use 24 centimetre cubes to build a cuboid which will fit on top of the shape.

   b Now describe it in the way shown by the **blue** writing.

3 **a** On squared paper, draw other shapes on which you can build a cuboid with 24 centimetre cubes.

   b Check your ideas using centimetre cubes.

   c Describe each cuboid.

CHALLENGE

- Make a cuboid with a volume of 50 cu cm.
- Describe it. • Try to draw it.

STEPS 4a:18

Building towers

interlocking centimetre cubes, RMA or 1 cm squared paper

This is a tower of centimetre cubes.

- **It has 4 centimetre cubes in each layer.**
- It has 2 layers.
- Its volume is 8 cu cm.

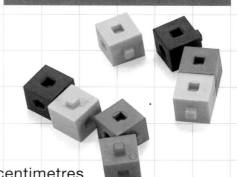

1   **a** Build this tower with centimetre cubes.
Then add more layers and count the cubic centimetres.

b Copy and complete this table.

number of layers	1	2	3	4	5	6	7	8	9	10
volume of the tower in cu cm	4	8								

2   Copy these shapes onto squared paper.

a   b   d

c

Build a tower with 36 centimetre cubes on each shape.
Record your results in the same way as in **1** .

CHALLENGE

Make towers shaped like the letters ⊔ and T,
each with a volume of 26 cu cm.

Multiple patterns

1 Mark the numbers on the 100-square like this.

   a Put a ◯ over the multiples of 3.

   b Put a ┼ over the multiples of 6.

   c Put a △ over the multiples of 9.

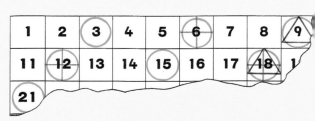

Numbers marked are common multiples of 3 and 6.

2 Write about the numbers marked like this.

   a   **b**   **c**

3 Write these numbers.

   a 6th multiple of 9   **b** 10th multiple of 3   **c** 8th multiple of 6
   d 9th multiple of 9   **e** 16th multiple of 3   **f** 13th multiple of 6
   g 11th multiple of 9   **h** 25th multiple of 3   **i** 16th multiple of 6

4 **a** List the numbers marked in ascending order.

   b Design a diagram like this
      for each of the numbers you found in **a**.

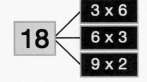

CHALLENGE

There are 6 common multiples of 3, 6 and 9 between 100 and 200.
True or false? Investigate.

Turning shapes

1   These shapes all have turning or rotational symmetry.
Think of a way to put them in order.

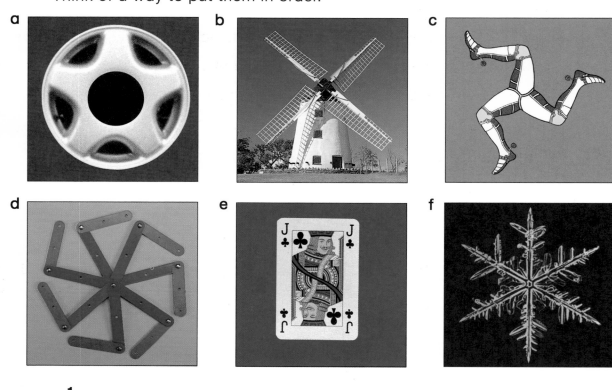

a   b   c

d   e   f

There is **½ turn clockwise** between these shapes.

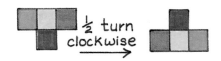

½ turn clockwise

2   Write the amount of turn **clockwise** between each pair of shapes.
Estimate before you check.

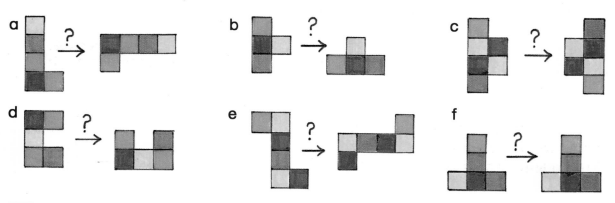

a   b   c

d   e   f

STEPS 4a:20

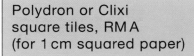

Polydron or Clixi
square tiles, RM A
(for 1 cm squared paper)

3 Write the amount of turn **anticlockwise** between each pair of shapes in **2**

4 Complete these sentences.

a $\frac{1}{4}$ turn clockwise is the same as ___ turn anticlockwise.

b $\frac{1}{2}$ turn clockwise is the same as ___ turn anticlockwise.

c $\frac{3}{4}$ turn clockwise is the same as ___ turn anticlockwise.

d 1 whole turn clockwise is the same as ___ turn anticlockwise.

5

Draw the missing shapes on squared paper.

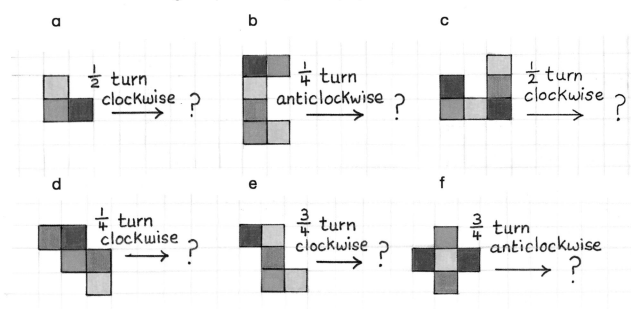

a $\frac{1}{2}$ turn clockwise ?

b $\frac{1}{4}$ turn anticlockwise ?

c $\frac{1}{2}$ turn clockwise ?

d $\frac{1}{4}$ turn clockwise ?

e $\frac{3}{4}$ turn clockwise ?

f $\frac{3}{4}$ turn anticlockwise ?

6 Choose and record shapes to go here.

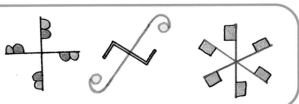

a $\frac{1}{4}$ turn clockwise ? ?

b $\frac{1}{2}$ turn anticlockwise ? ?

c $\frac{3}{4}$ turn anticlockwise ? ?

CHALLENGE

Design 'doodle' patterns like these
with turning symmetry
but no line symmetry.

Turning symmetry

I made these with Pattern Blocks and then copied them on to paper.

I made turning symmetry patterns using shape and letter stencils.

1   Create and record your own patterns with turning symmetry.
    Choose materials to help you.

6-spike numbers

6-spike abacus, 6 beads, RM 80

Work with a friend if you can.

I put six beads on this abacus to show an odd number between 10 000 and 20 000.

I drew the beads on RM 80 and wrote the number.

12 003

1   Use 6 beads, a 6-spike abacus and RM 80.
Find and record a number which is:

a a 4-digit number with no zeros in it

b a 5-digit number with a zero in the thousands column

c an even number between 40 000 and 50 000

d the smallest even number

e the smallest 6-digit number

f the largest 5-digit odd number

g the smallest 5-digit number ending in '000'

h the largest 5-digit number ending in '000'.

CHALLENGE

Fit these 4 loose spikes on the abacus
in different ways to find twelve **5-digit odd numbers**.

Draw each abacus and write the number it shows.

Numbers in place

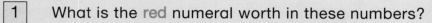

In the number on my T-shirt, the **red** numeral is worth 600.

13 672

1 What is the **red** numeral worth in these numbers?

a
24569

b
19 326

c
62 854

d
16 999

2 Write the next three numbers in these sequences.

a 8 500   9 000   9 500   ___ ___ ___

b 11 211   12 211   13 211   ___ ___ ___

c 5 000   10 000   15 000   ___ ___ ___

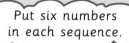

Put six numbers in each sequence.

3 Write sequences of 5-digit numbers.

a Count back in five hundreds   ___ ___ ___ ___ ___ ___

b Count back in thousands   ___ ___ ___ ___ ___ ___

c Count back in five thousands   ___ ___ ___ ___ ___ ___

4 Write a 5-digit number with:

a 8 in the thousands position   **b** 5 in the hundreds position

c 2 in the ten-thousands position   **d** 1 in the tens position.

Write the number which is ...

5

10 less than:
a 72 000
b 62 110
c 19 483
d 33 333

6
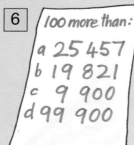
100 more than:
a 25 457
b 19 821
c 9 900
d 99 900

7

1000 less than:
a 11 111
b 24 680
c 10 001
d 99 999

8

10 000 more than:
a 55
b 127
c 2468
d 12 914

STEPS 4a:21

Working with numbers

calculator

1 Copy and complete.

    a 14 500 is the same as ⬡ tens or ⬡ hundreds.
    b 16 000 is the same as ⬡ thousands or ⬡ hundreds or ⬡ tens.

2 18 249 can be written in expanded form like this: $10\,000 + 8\,000 + 200 + 40 + 9$.

    Write these in expanded form.

    a 23 417   **b** 16 100   **c** 21 310   **d** 19 004   **e** 13 040   **f** 100 020

3 Write what you need to **add** to this number ⟶ `24678.`
to make your calculator display show:

    a `25678.`   **b** `24688.`   **c** `24978.`

    d `27678.`   **e** `24679.`   **f** `44678.`

4 Write what you need to **subtract** from this ⟶ `15769.`
number to make the calculator show:

    a `5769.`   **b** `11769.`   **c** `15709.`

    d `15760.`   **e** `15469.`   **f** `10769.`

5 Make 10 statements
using these numbers and **>**.

    23 164   23 416   23 146   23 461   23 641

> One statement is
> 23 164 **>** 23 146.

CHALLENGE

Enter `198762.` on your calculator.

Record how you can change the display to `0.` using:

a 2 subtractions   **b** 3 subtractions   **c** 4 subtractions   **d** 5 subtractions.

Probability line ■ ■ ■

scissors, glue pen, RM 87

A **probability line** can be used to show how likely an event is to happen. It is always numbered from 0 to 1.

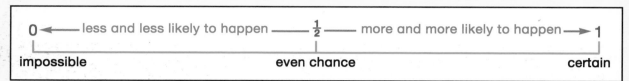

0 ◄— less and less likely to happen —— $\frac{1}{2}$ —— more and more likely to happen —► 1

impossible   even chance   certain

Work with a friend if you like.

1. Cut out the 12 statement cards on RM 87.

2. On a long strip of paper, make a probability number line like the one shown below.

3. Decide where on the scale is the most sensible place to put the statements.

You can glue the cards down and draw lines to where you think they best fit on the line.

We've put this statement very near **0** because it's **very unlikely** to happen.

The Queen will come to my house tomorrow.

0 impossible   even chance   certai

CHALLENGE

Make cards to put at these positions on the scale.

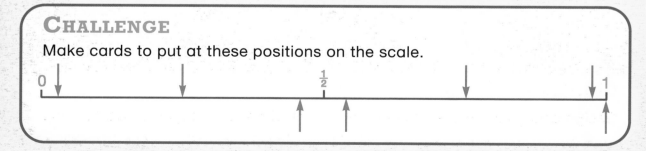

0                              $\frac{1}{2}$ 1

What's the chance?

This probability line is numbered 0·5 instead of ½.

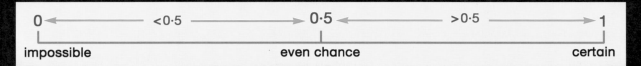

1 For this spinner, write **0**, **0·5** or **1** to show the chance of spinning:
  a red   **b** green   **c** yellow

2 Write **0**, **0·5** or **1** to show the chance of spinning:
  a green   **b** yellow   **c** red

For the spinners below, write **0**, **<0·5**, **0·5**, **>0·5** or **1** to show the chance of spinning:

3 **a** red
    b green
    c yellow

4 **a** red
    b green
    c yellow

5 **a** red
    b green
    c yellow

6 **a** red
    b green
    c yellow

CHALLENGE

Design and colour more spinners. Write the chance of spinning each colour.

Four-in-a-line

15 counters each
(2 colours), calculator

A game for two players

- Share this board and take turns to play.
- On your turn, point to a division problem in one of the hexagons. Read it aloud and say the answer.
- Your partner checks your answer on the calculator.
- If you were right, put a counter on that hexagon.
- Now your partner chooses a problem.
- Clear the display after each check.
- The first player to get 4 counters in a line wins.

6÷6=	64÷8=	90÷9=	48÷6=	32÷8=
72÷9=	80÷8=	24÷6=	40÷8=	63÷9=
30÷6=	16÷8=	54÷6=	9÷9=	81÷9=
18÷9=	8÷8=	36÷6=	27÷9=	54÷9=
56÷8=	45÷9=	12÷6=	48÷8=	42÷6=
60÷6=	72÷8=	24÷8=	18÷6=	36÷9=

STEPS 4a:23

Class groups

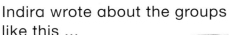

Mrs Hall grouped 20 children in 5s.
How many groups?

Indira wrote about the groups
like this ...

$$5\overline{)20}$$
$$\underline{-20} \quad (4 \text{ groups of } 5)$$
$$0 \quad \text{left over}$$

... **then** she wrote the answer
above the line

$$5\overline{)20}^{\,4 \text{ groups}}$$
$$\underline{-20} \quad (4 \text{ groups of } 5)$$
$$0 \quad \text{left over}$$

1   Use Indira's way to work out how many groups there will be.

    a   16 children grouped in 2s   **b**   24 children grouped in 4s
    c   45 children grouped in 5s   **d**   36 children grouped in 6s
    e   21 children grouped in 3s   **f**   90 children grouped in 10s
    g   72 children grouped in 8s   **h**   54 children grouped in 9s

Ravi wrote the answer like this: $5\overline{)20}^{\,4}$

2   Use Ravi's way to record the answers to these.

    a $20 \div 2$ **b** $32 \div 4$ **c** $18 \div 3$ **d** $40 \div 8$
    e $35 \div 5$ **f** $30 \div 6$ **g** $27 \div 3$ **h** $70 \div 10$
    i $40 \div 4$ **j** $30 \div 5$ **k** $81 \div 9$ **l** $64 \div 8$
    m $45 \div 9$ **n** $54 \div 6$ **o** $28 \div 4$

Find six different answers for each 'missing numbers' division.

No answer should have a remainder.

CHALLENGE

a

b

c

Grouping with remainders

Jenny and Rob have a farm shop.
One day, Jenny packed 27 eggs into boxes.
She put six in each box.

One way to show what she did
is to divide like this ...

$6\overline{)27}$ eggs
$-\underline{24}$ (4 boxes of 6 eggs)
   3 eggs remaining

... then to write the answer above
the line.

   4 remainder 3
$6\overline{)27}$ eggs
$-\underline{24}$ (4 boxes of 6 eggs)
   3 eggs remaining

1 Work out how many egg boxes
she will fill and how many eggs
will be left over each day if she
starts with this number of eggs.

	Day	Eggs
a	Monday	19
b	Tuesday	57
c	Wednesday	40
d	Thursday	29
e	Friday	45
f	Saturday	56
g	Sunday	34

2 Rob packs the fruit and vegetables.
Work out how many full packs he can make
and how many will be left over.

a 27 carrots packed in 4s   b 42 courgettes packed in 5s
c 47 apples packed in 6s   d 19 swedes packed in 2s
e 28 leeks packed in 3s   f 38 tomatoes packed in 8s
g 86 onions packed in 10s   h 60 plums packed in 9s

CHALLENGE

Write a story which ends like this.

and so Jenny and Rob ended up
with 8 boxes of eggs and 4 eggs left over.

Division stories

Find the answers to these in your own way.
Show how you work out the answers.
Then copy and complete
the **yellow** sentences.

a Jan's mum cut 19 m of curtain fabric
into 2 m lengths.

   She cut _____ lengths
   and had _____ m of fabric left over.

b Jan had 54 snap cards.
She dealt them out equally
between herself and her 5 friends.

   They got _____ cards each.

   c Jan's dad spent 48p on 6p stamps.

   He bought _____ 6p stamps
   and had _____ p change from £5.

d Jan's brother Sam was sorting out his tapes.
He had 80. He gave 8 to Jan and put the rest
in boxes, 9 in each box.

   He put _____ tapes in boxes and needed
   _____ boxes.

e Jan made fudge for the school fair.
She made 4 trays of fudge,
with 48 pieces in each tray.
She put 8 pieces of fudge in bags
until the fudge ran out.

   She made _____ bags of fudge for the fair.

f Jan's dad bought apples in packs of 8
and oranges in packs of 6 for her party.
Altogether, he had 48 pieces of fruit.

   He bought _____ apples and _____ oranges.

Working with money

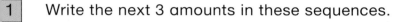

1 Write the next 3 amounts in these sequences.

  a £2·70   £2·90   £3·10   _____   _____   _____
  b £9·25   £9·75   £10·25   _____   _____   _____
  c £0·50   £5·50   £10·50   _____   _____   _____

2 Copy and complete this table.

£	£6·10		£10			£0·07	£2·94		£8·23	
p	610p	508p		51p	950p			770p		1110p

3 Write all the different amounts you can make using 4 of these coins and notes.

4 Write these amounts in order of size, smallest first.

5 Liam has been using a calculator and working in £s.
How much money is represented by these displays?

  a `5.`   **b** `0.35`   **c** `8.1`

  d `0.09`   **e** `7.7`   **f** `0.5`

CHALLENGE

Investigate ways to make these amounts using **4** coins each time.

£1·20   £1·25   £1·30   £1·35   £1·40   £1·45 ...

How much?

Show how you work out the answers.

1 Karen saved this amount of money
to buy a magic set.
She needs £3·46 more before she can buy it.
What is the cost of the magic set?

2 Bridget and Pat together bought a present for their grandad.
Bridget gave this amount.   Pat gave this amount.

What did the present cost?

3 Louise had this amount in her purse.   Her mother added this amount.

How much money is in her purse now?

4 Donald had £4·50 in his money box. He put in four more coins
and now has £8. Which four coins did he put in?

5 Fiona had six matching coins in her hand. Her mother gave her
£7 more to buy a £10 watch. Which six coins did she start with?

6 Find the missing amounts of money.

a £3 · 14   b £6 · 47   c £7 · 45   d £■ · ■■
  + £5 · 79   + £3 · 85   + £■ · ■■   + £4 · 15
  ─────────   ─────────   £9 · 69   £8 · 99

CHALLENGE

Eight pairs of numbers can be written
in the ■ and ▲ places. What are they?

£5 · 2 3
+ £2 · ■ 6
─────────
£7 · ▲ 9

Subtracting money

Show how you work out the answers.

1. Anil saved this amount of money.
He spent £4·15 on a game.
How much of his savings is left?

2. Zoe paid for a scale model with a £10 note.
She got this amount of change.
How much did the model cost?

3. Ian's mum had £9·68 in her purse.
She lent this amount to Ian.
How much did she have left in her purse?

4. Ela's grandad bought her felt pens costing £1·80.
He was given a £5 note and four coins
change from £10.
Which four coins were in his change?

5. Nick had £8·75 to spend on presents.
He used three coins to buy
a pencil case and had £6·25 left.
Which three coins did he use?

6. Find the missing amounts of money.

a	b	c	d	e	f
£9 · 47	£7 · 82	£8 · 46	£■ · ■■	£5 · 00	£9 · 19
− £2 · 52	− £1 · 54	− £5 · 85	− £1 · 25	− £■ · ■■	− £■ · ■■
			£5 · 85	£1 · 47	£3 · 65

CHALLENGE

Part of the price of these books is missing.
The difference in price is £1·72.
What prices might the books be?

£2·

£3·

School play

Emma buys 4 tickets. Each costs 40p.
She can work out the total cost by:

adding   or   multiplying

adding	multiplying
40p	40
40p	x 4
40p	
+ 40p	160p
160p	160p is the same as £1·60

OAKWOOD SCHOOL

TICKETS
Adults   75p
Children   55p
Senior Citizens 40p

REFRESHMENTS
Tea 20p
Coffee 25p
Cold drinks 30p
Biscuit 15p
Cake 25p

Don't use a calculator but
use notes and coins
if you like.

Write your answers in pounds.
For example: £1·35

1 Find the total cost of tickets for each group.

   a 4 adults   **b** 3 children   **c** 10 senior citizens

2 What is the total cost of:

   a 5 adults' tickets **and** 3 teas?
   b 2 senior citizens' tickets **and** 2 coffees **and** 2 cakes?
   c 4 children's tickets **and** 4 cold drinks **and** 4 cakes?
   d 3 adults' tickets **and** 3 coffees **and** 3 biscuits?
   e 1 senior citizen's ticket and 2 adult tickets **and** 2 children's tickets?

I have an amount of money,
between 50p and £1.
If I multiply it by 6,
I get the same answer
as if I added £3.

CHALLENGE

What is the amount of money?

Sharing the cost

Kiwi fruit
10 for £1·50

Pomegranates
4 for £2·20

Oranges
5 for £1·25

Apples
3 for 90p

Grapefruit
5 for £2

Bananas
4 for £1

Pears
3 for £0·96

Mangoes
2 for £1·70

1 Use coins and notes. Find the cost of **1** of each of these.

    a kiwi fruit   **b** mangoes   **c** apples   **d** pears

    e grapefruit   **f** bananas   **g** oranges   **h** pomegranates

2 At the end of the day some fruit was sold at **half price**.
What was the new price of:

    a 10 kiwi fruit   **b** 3 apples   **c** 4 bananas   **d** 4 pomegranates?

CHALLENGE

- Get £2.40 in notes and coins.
  Investigate ways to share the amount between 2,3,4,5,6 … up to 12 people.

- Which 'sharings' have coins left over? • Make a chart of what you find out.

Distance and direction

RM 98,
16 mm counter

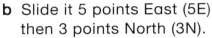 If you need to revise co-ordinates, look at page 37.

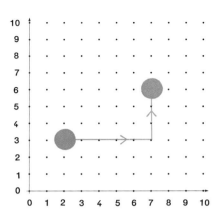

1
   a Put a counter on point (2,3) on the grid on RM 98.

   b Slide it 5 points East (5E) then 3 points North (3N).

 Check that you have finished on point (7,6).

2 Slide the counter 5E then 3N starting on these points.
Write where you finish each time.

   a (1,1)   **b** (5,2)   **c** (4,7)   **d** (5,6)
   e (3,3)   **f** (0,7)   **g** (2,0)   **h** (0,0)

3 Start on point (5,6) each time.
Write where you finish if you slide the counter like this.

   a 5W then 2S   **b** 4N then 4E   **c** 4E then 6S   **d** 3S then 5W
   e 2E then 4N   **f** 2N then 3W   **g** 6S then 5W   **h** 4N then 4E

CHALLENGE

 It could finish on (2,7).

- Always start with your counter on point (5,5).

- Slide the counter N, S, E or W to a new position **5 points away**.

- List the co-ordinates of all the new positions the counter can finish on.

Translating patterns

Pattern Blocks,
shape templates, A3 paper

Tom followed the instructions on this card.
He made a pattern by ruling a line, sliding
the shape along it and drawing round it.
Then he coloured part of the pattern.

Use:

Direction of slide:
Distance between points: 3·5 cm
Number of outlines: 4

1 Copy and colour Tom's pattern.

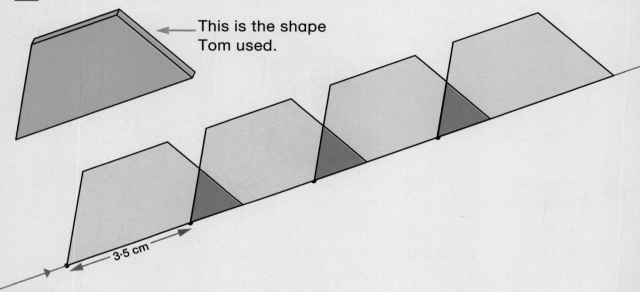

This is the shape
Tom used.

3·5 cm

2 Construct sliding patterns using these cards.

a

Use:

Direction of slide:
Distance between points: 3·5 cm
Number of outlines: 6

b

Use:

Direction of slide:
Distance between points: 2·5 cm
Number of outlines: 7

c

Use:

Direction of slide:
Distance between points: 1·5 cm
Number of outlines: 10

d

Use:

Direction of slide:
Distance between points: 2·2 cm
Number of outlines: 8

3 **a** Use any templates to design your own sliding patterns.
  b Write an instruction card for each design.

Skeleton shapes

'Translate' means 'slide' or 'move in a straight line'.

1 Draw a skeleton cuboid like this:

a Draw the outline of an oblong.

b Translate it to a new position.

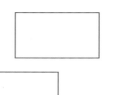

c Join matching points with straight lines to construct a cuboid.

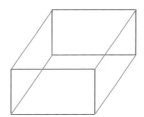

d Try again but make the oblongs overlap.

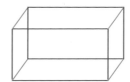

2 Start with an equilateral triangle each time.
Try to draw different triangular prisms.

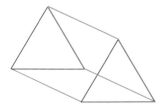

3 Try translating other polygons in the same way and joining them to make different skeleton shapes.

CHALLENGE

Try constructing strange 'tunnels' like these.

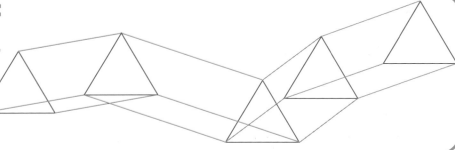

Birthdays

1 How many years old this year
is someone born in January ...

a 1992?   **b** 1989?   **c** 1975?   **d** 1960?

> Use this date-line
> to help you.

2 Work out which year you will have these birthdays.

3 Here are four people's birthdays.

Amul 4th January
Becky 4th April
Chris 4th May
Dana 4th October

> Take care!
> There are 2 answers
> to each question.
> Find them both.

Find and record how many months
there are between these people's birthdays.

a Amul and Becky   **b** Amul and Dana
c Chris and Dana   **d** Dana and Becky

4 Write what day of the week it will be:

a 5 days after Wednesday
b 7 days after Monday
c 14 days after Thursday
d 6 days before Saturday
e 9 days before Friday
f 21 days before Tuesday.

5 There are 365 days in a year. How many weeks are there in a year?
(**Hint:** the answer is **not** 52!)

STEPS 4a:26

Hiking times

Morgan, Sharon, Jake and Amy took part in a sponsored hike.
This chart shows their times at the checkpoints.

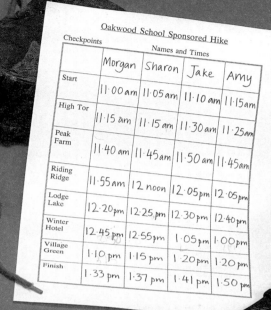

Oakwood School Sponsored Hike

Checkpoints	Names and Times			
	Morgan	Sharon	Jake	Amy
Start	11·00 am	11·05 am	11·10 am	11·15 am
High Tor	11·15 am	11·15 am	11·30 am	11·25 am
Peak Farm	11·40 am	11·45 am	11·50 am	11·45 am
Riding Ridge	11·55 am	12 noon	12·05 pm	12·05 pm
Lodge Lake	12·20 pm	12·25 pm	12·30 pm	12·40 pm
Winter Hotel	12·45 pm	12·55 pm	1·05 pm	1·00 pm
Village Green	1·10 pm	1·15 pm	1·20 pm	1·20 pm
Finish	1·33 pm	1·37 pm	1·41 pm	1·50 pm

1 How long after Sharon started did Amy start?

2 Who reached High Tor in the shortest time?

3 How much time did Jake take to reach Riding Ridge?

4 Who took the longest time to reach Lodge Lake?

5 The path from Peak Farm to Winter Hotel was rocky.
Who was the fastest on that part?

6 Who did the whole hike in:

   a the shortest time   b the longest time?

7 For how long did each child walk:

   a in the morning   b in the afternoon?

CHALLENGE

Each of them stopped for a rest on one of the stages.
Decide which stage it might have been for each person
and explain your choice.

Travelling by train

This diagram shows Inter City train routes
from London to Manchester
and London to Wolverhampton.
It tells you the times taken by a train
from London to reach each station.

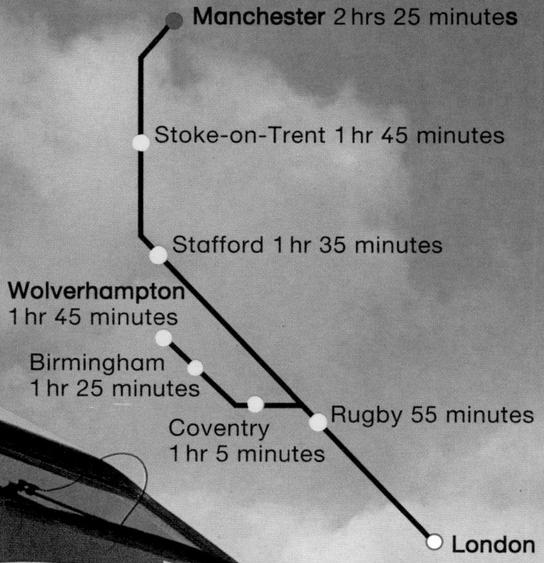

> A train leaving London at 07:30
> will arrive in Manchester
> 2 hours and 25 minutes later, at 09:55

Manchester 2 hrs 25 minutes

Stoke-on-Trent 1 hr 45 minutes

Stafford 1 hr 35 minutes

Wolverhampton
1 hr 45 minutes

Birmingham
1 hr 25 minutes

Rugby 55 minutes

Coventry
1 hr 5 minutes

London

1 Copy and complete these timetables.

a

London	13:05
Rugby	
Stafford	14:40
Stoke-on-Trent	
Manchester	

b

London	
Rugby	18:15
Coventry	
Birmingham	
Wolverhampton	19:05

2

a You want to be in Manchester by 12:00.
Which is the **latest** train you could catch?

b Some friends will join the train
at Stoke-on-Trent.
What time does your train get there?

c What time will you reach Manchester?

Departures from London
to Manchester

08:45
09:15
09:50
10:25

74

STEPS 4a:26

Rod problems

Here are the Cuisenaire Rods, drawn **half-scale**, with their colours and lengths.

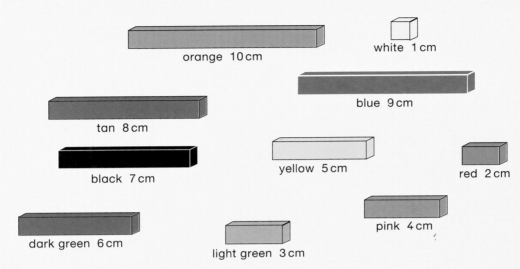

orange 10 cm

white 1 cm

blue 9 cm

tan 8 cm

black 7 cm

yellow 5 cm

red 2 cm

dark green 6 cm

light green 3 cm

pink 4 cm

- Work out the answers to these problems **without** using real rods.

- Write down what you do to show your teacher.

- **Afterwards**, check with rods and a metre rule, if you want.

1 Find the total length these will make, fitted end to end.

    a 3 red and 4 black rods   **b** 5 pink and 2 blue rods
    c 8 tan rods and 5 light green rods   **d** 6 orange and 5 dark green rods
    e 9 yellow and 5 blue rods   **f** 8 black and 4 blue rods
    g 9 light green and 8 dark green rods **h** 7 yellow and 7 pink rods

2 Each set of these rods, fitted end to end, will equal 64 cm.
    Find the missing number or colour in each set.

    a 5 tan and ..... light green rods   **b** ..... tan and 8 pink rods
    c ..... orange and 7 red rods   **d** 4 .... and 6 dark green rods
    e 6 blue and 5 .... rods   **f** ..... black and 3 yellow rods

CHALLENGE

Find the missing numbers or colours.
- 7 ...... and 3 ...... rods equal 42 cm.
- ... yellow and ... green rods equal 43 cm.

Sticker sums

5mm squared paper or RMC

Here are 14 rows of 6 stickers.
If you tear the stickers into two at the green arrow,
you will have 4 rows of 6 stickers
and 10 rows of 6 stickers.

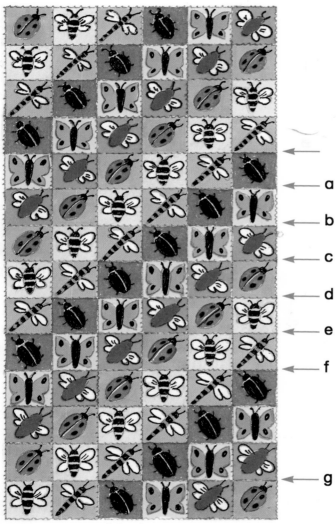

← a
← b
← c
← d
← e
← f
← g

14 × 6 = 84

You can write about the two parts like this.

$(4 \times 6) + (10 \times 6)$
$= 24 + 60$
$= 84$

1 Write about the two parts each time if you tear the stickers at the red arrows.

2 Write which example you found hardest. Why?

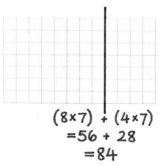

$(8 \times 7) + (4 \times 7)$
$= 56 + 28$
$= 84$

3 Draw 6 more rectangles like this on squared paper to show different ways of splitting the rows.

76

Finding products

Here is a way to help you find or check answers to problems like 23 × 5.

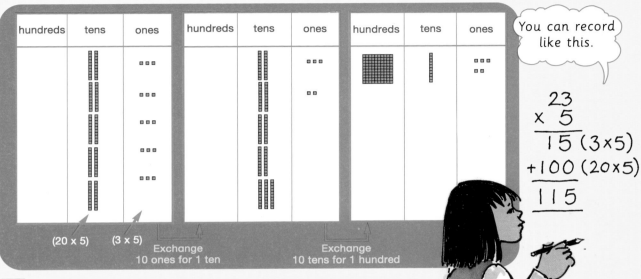

You can record like this.

$$\begin{array}{r} 23 \\ \times\ 5 \\ \hline 15\ (3\times5) \\ +100\ (20\times5) \\ \hline 115 \end{array}$$

1 Find the value of these pieces.
Write your answers as multiplications.

a 7 sets of these:

b 6 sets of these:

c 8 sets of these:

d 5 sets of these:

e 4 sets of these:

f 9 sets of these:

2 Find these products.

a 14 × 5   **b** 26 × 6   **c** 33 × 4   **d** 18 × 8
e 19 × 3   **f** 35 × 6   **g** 28 × 7   **h** 13 × 9

CHALLENGE

Fit these numbers into this frame: ×

2   **3**   **4**   **5**

Try to find the 4 possible **odd-numbered** products.

Toy shop

Mrs O'Neill bought Christmas stock for her toy shop. These are the numbers of toys she bought and the prices she charged.

1   Work out how much money she took when she sold these.

a 3 at £17

b 7 at £13

c 6 at £28

d 5 at £16

e 4 at £14

f 5 at £15

g 7 at £35

h 9 at £13

i 8 at £12

2   Work out how many items are in each set of packs.

a 6 packs

b 9 packs 12 finger puppets

c 8 packs 16 felt tip pens

d 7 packs 8 masks

CHALLENGE

If Mrs O'Neill sold **all** the toys in ⬜1⬜, she would take between £900 and £1000. True or false?

6 x 6 pinboard,
elastic bands, RM F

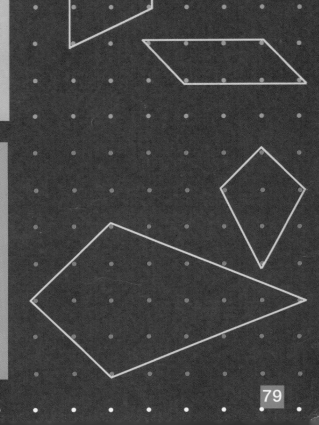

A trapezium has one pair of parallel sides.

Two are shown here.

1   Make five more on your pinboard
and record each one on RM F.
Write **trapezium** beneath each one.

A parallelogram has both pairs
or opposite sides parallel.

Two are shown here.

2   Make five more and record them
in the same way as in 1 .

A kite has two pairs of equal sides
next to each other.

Two are shown here.

3   Make five more and record them
in the same way.

Diagonals

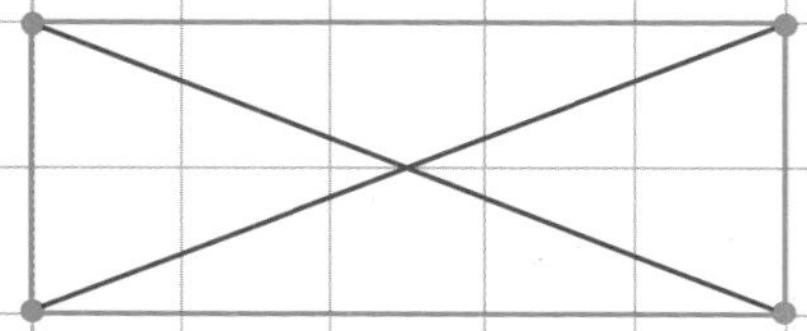

This drawing shows
a **quadrilateral**
with its **diagonals**.

Predict what the
finished shape will be
before you draw the sides.

1 | Copy these diagonals
and draw the four sides
around them.

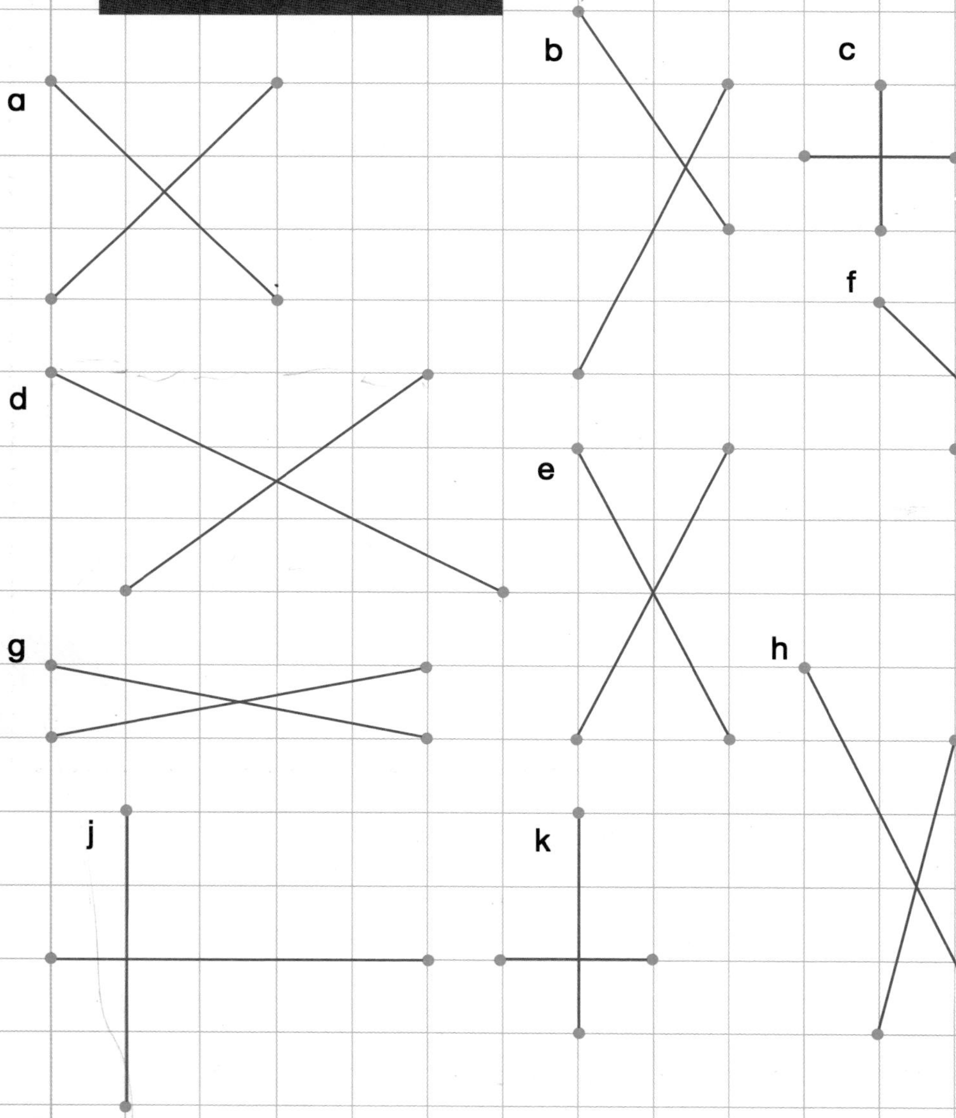

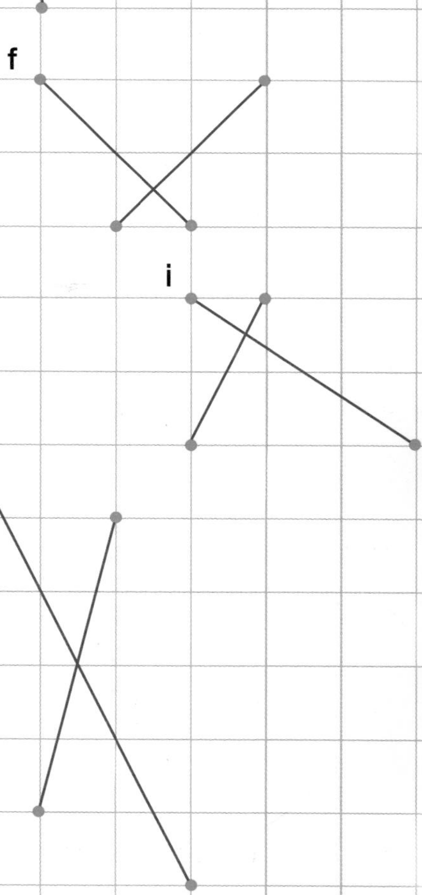

a

b

c

d

e

f

g

h

i

j

k

80

1 cm triangular
dotty paper (RM G)

2   Underneath each shape, **a** to **k**, write one of these names.

  square   oblong   trapezium   **rhombus**   kite   **parallelogram**

3   Now do these in the same way on triangular dotty paper.

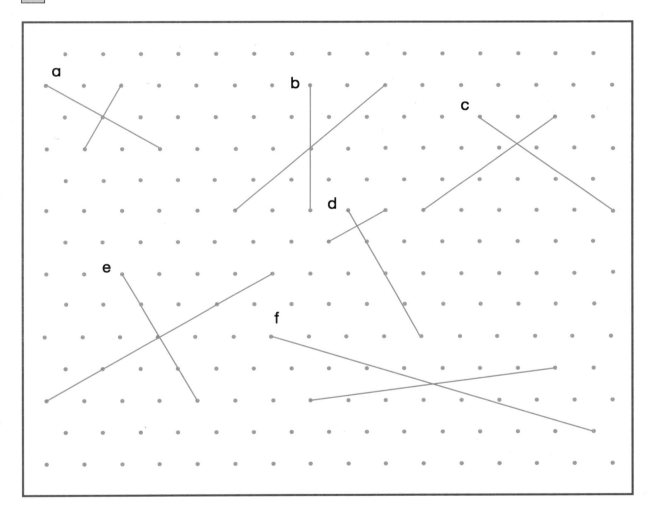

4   Decide the best way to find out if this is true.

All squares have diagonals like this one.

Write down what you do to show your teacher.

Quadrilateral angles

paper quadrilaterals, scissors

Zena named the four angles of this quadrilateral a, b, c and d.

The she tore it into four pieces around its corners.

She found that the angles fitted together in a full turn without gaps or overlaps.

She glued them down to show her teacher.

> I think that the angles of **any** quadrilateral will be equal to a full turn.

1   Experiment with different quadrilaterals to find out if what Zena thinks is true.

2   Afterwards, write down what you discover.

82

Do-the-same machines

Mick and Molly both fed 5, 7, 2, 8 and 6 into machines and made input/output tables.

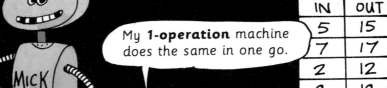

Look! I've made a **2-operation** machine.

My **1-operation** machine does the same in one go.

IN	MIDDLE	OUT
5	8	15
7	10	17
2	5	12
8	11	18
6	9	16

IN	OUT
5	15
7	17
2	12
8	18
6	16

1 **a** Design an input/output table like Mick's for this **2-operation** machine.

   b Design a **1-operation** machine and its table to do the same job.

2 **a** Design an input/output table for this machine.

   b Design a **2-operation subtraction** machine which does the same job.

   c Design a table for your new machine.

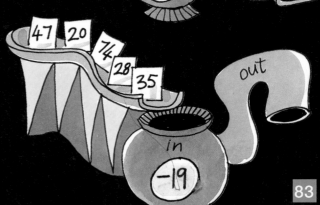

More machines

Here is one way to record what these machines do.

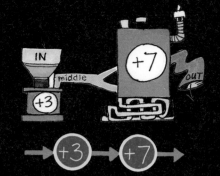 

1   Record, in the same way, how a **1-operation** machine will do these.

a ⟶ (+20) ⟶ (-10)

b ⟶ (-6) ⟶ (+14)

c ⟶ (+4) ⟶ (+13)

d ⟶ (-16) ⟶ (-9)

e ⟶ (-12) ⟶ (-4)

f ⟶ (+8) ⟶ (-4) ⟶ (+3)

g ⟶ (-3) ⟶ (-4) ⟶ (-5)

h ⟶ (+5) ⟶ (-10) ⟶ (+5)

2   Check your answers to **1** by feeding in 3 different numbers.

My answer to 1a
was ⟶ (+10) ⟶
This is how I checked it.

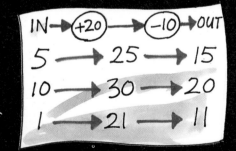

IN ⟶ (+20) ⟶ (-10) ⟶ OUT

5 ⟶ 25 ⟶ 15

10 ⟶ 30 ⟶ 20

1 ⟶ 21 ⟶ 11

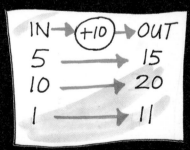

IN ⟶ (+10) ⟶ OUT

5 ⟶ 15

10 ⟶ 20

1 ⟶ 11

CHALLENGE

If you use numerals from 0 to 10
on the dotted lines here,
you can find **8 different ways** to do
the same job as this machine.
True or false? Investigate.

Back to the start

Look at this back-to-the-start machine.

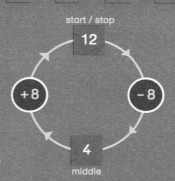

1   Make three more like it
using + 8 and – 8 in the same way.

2   Copy machines **a**, **b**, and **c** three times each.

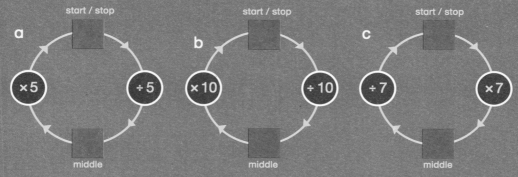

Complete the machines by filling in the rectangles with these numbers.

2   4   7   10   20   28   35   49   70   100

3   Complete these machines so that any output number
will be the same as its input number.

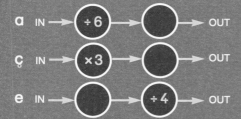

4   For each machine in **3**, complete a table
like this one for **3 a**, to check if you are correct.

Choose 3 numbers
to put in.
I've done one for you!

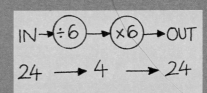

IN →÷6→×6→OUT
24 → 4 → 24

Scrambled alphabet

1. Complete grid **a** on RM 111 to code the alphabet.

In this code
A is 5 and T is 43 ...
so AT is 5,43.
I wonder if there is
a pattern to this code?

2. Use the code to unscramble this joke.

Question:
49, 19, 13, 39, 13   11, 33   29, 33, 31, 25, 13, 53, 41
9, 33, 33, 25   43, 19, 13, 21, 39   15, 33, 33, 11?

Answer:
45, 31, 11, 13, 39   5   17, 33, 39, 21, 27, 27, 5.

3. Write your favourites in code.
   a food   **b** colour   **c** game

4. **a** In secret, work out a coded alphabet
   of your own, using grid **b** on RM 111.
   Write a joke in your code.

   b Give a friend your coded joke
   and a copy of the lines you wrote
   for A, B and C.

This is what
I gave my friend.

A	1	3	10
B	2	6	13
C	3	9	16

   c Can your friend unscramble
   your code and read your joke?
   (If your friend is stuck,
   think of another clue.)

| | change to numbers | x 2 | + 3 |
	IN		OUT
A	1	2	5
B	2	4	
C	3		
D			
E			
F			
G			
H			
I			
J			
K			
L			
M			
N			
O			
P			
Q			
R			
S			
T	20	40	43
U			
V			
W			
X			
Y			
Z			

Sevens and division

Some of this rectangle
is hidden under the **blue** paper. ⟶
The top row has an area of 7 sq cm.

1   Write how many rows long the
rectangle will be if it has an area of:

     a 56 sq cm   **b** 35 sq cm
     c 21 sq cm   **d** 70 sq cm
     e 49 sq cm   **f** 28 sq cm
     g 42 sq cm   **h** 63 sq cm.

2   Rewrite the speech bubbles so that
the blue numbers are correct.

     a

> There are 63 days
> in **8** weeks.

     b

> If there are 35 ml
> of medicine left, that
> will make **six** 5 ml spoonfuls.

3   Write the missing numbers.

     a ⬛ $\div 7 = 6$ **b** $14 \div$ ⬛ $= 2$ **c** $35 \div 7 =$ ⬛   **d** $63 \div 7 =$ ⬛
     e $21 \div 7 =$ ⬛   **f** ⬛ $\div 7 = 4$ **g** $49 \div$ ⬛ $= 7$ **h** ⬛ $\div 7 = 8$

4   Copy and complete these division patterns.

     a   Start ⟶

$$7 \div 1 = 7$$
$$= 7$$

       Finish ⟶

$$70 \div 10 = 7$$

     b   Start ⟶

$$70 \div 7 = 10$$

       Finish ⟶

$$7 \div 7 = 1$$

5   Write a sharing story for this division. $28 \div 7$

CHALLENGE

Put multiples of 7 between 70 and 150
into this machine.

Try to find all the pairs of input and output cards.

Polygon divisions

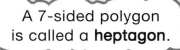

A 7-sided polygon is called a **heptagon**.

1 Write how many heptagons you could make with this number of straws.

a 14 **b** 56 **c** 21 **d** 49 **e** 35 **f** 63

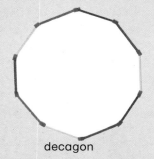

decagon

nonagon

2 Copy and complete these sentences.
Show any workings-out for each sentence.

a 28 straws make ..... triangles with   ..... left over.

b 45 straws make ..... hexagons with ..... left over.

c 54 straws make ..... pentagons with ..... left over.

d 69 straws make ..... octagons with   ..... left over.

e 54 straws make ..... heptagons with ..... left over.

f 85 straws make ..... decagons with ..... left over.

g 60 straws make ..... nonagons with ..... left over.

3 Write a sharing story for this division. **40 ÷ 7**

4 Work out the answers to these in your own way.

a 23 ÷ 3   **b** 39 ÷ 4   **c** 47 ÷ 5   **d** 59 ÷ 9

5 Look for clues to help you complete these.

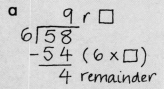

a
```
     9 r ☐
6 ⟌ 5 8
  - 5 4  (6 × ☐)
      4 remainder
```

b
```
     ☐ r ☐
7 ⟌ 4 1
  - 3 5  (7 × ☐)
      ☐ remainder
```

c
```
     ☐ r 5
8 ⟌ 6 9
  - ☐☐  (☐ × ☐)
      5 remainder
```

STEPS 4a:30

Division problems

Find the answers to these. Show how you work out the answers.

1

a To play a game, Ms Ross asked
4 children to share a box of 60 logic blocks.
How many blocks did each get?

b Ms Ross ordered 120 coloured pencils
for her class. These were packed in boxes of 8.
How many boxes did she order?

c Ms Ross gave 4 interlocking triangles
to each child to make a tetrahedron.
She gave out 76 triangles.
How many children made a tetrahedron?

d Jack told Ms Ross he had used 5 g weights
to balance a packet weighing 95 g.
How many 5 g weights did he use?

e Ms Ross bought a packet of 96 beans
for the class garden.
The beans were planted in rows of 8.
How many rows were there?

f The children helped Ms Ross
to plant daffodils, 6 in a pot.
**If 84 daffodils were planted,
how many pots were needed?**

g Ms Ross said, 'Christmas Day
will be in 98 days'.
How many weeks is that?

CHALLENGE

Make up sharing and grouping problems for others to work out.
The answers must be between 10 and 20 with no remainders.

Sponsored swim

Castle School had a sponsored swim for charity.

Kelly is a strong swimmer and swam 50 lengths.

Now she wants to collect her sponsor money using this form.

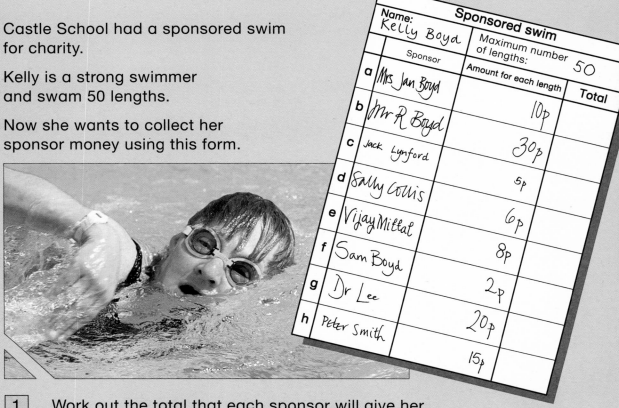

	Sponsored swim		
Name: Kelly Boyd		**Maximum number of lengths:** 50	
	Sponsor	Amount for each length	Total
a	Mrs Jan Boyd		
b	Mr R Boyd	10p	
c	Jack Lynford	30p	
d	Sally Collis	5p	
e	Vijay Mittal	6p	
f	Sam Boyd	8p	
g	Dr Lee	2p	
h	Peter Smith	20p	
		15p	

1   Work out the total that each sponsor will give her.

2   Work out how much money she will raise altogether.

3   Children who could swim up to 10 lengths took part
in a team swim totalling 30 lengths.
Work out the missing numbers in the table for each team of 4.

team a	Anna	Dan	Simon	Gaby
lengths swum	7	8		6

team d	Justin	Ed	Jim	Michael
lengths swum	6		6	9

team b	Elaine	Paul	Meena	Andrew
lengths swum	8	7	5	

team e	Robert	Ruth	Sewa	David
lengths swum	9	5		8

team c	Cathy	Jung	Vicky	Nancy
lengths swum	9	4		7

team f	Sarah	Richard	Alice	Mark
lengths swum		2	8	10

The 6 teams raised these amounts ⟶
for swimming the 30 lengths.

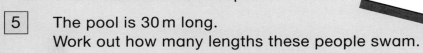

team	amount raised
a	£45
b	£60
c	£36
d	£63
e	£48
f	£54

4 Work out the amount each team
was sponsored for swimming a length.
Use a calculator if it helps.

5 The pool is 30 m long.
Work out how many lengths these people swam.

   a Gerry swam 330 m   **b** Hannah swam 450 m
   c Zak swam 270 m   **d** Polly swam 900 m
   e Maggie swam 510 m   **f** Tariq swam 600 m

6 If they started at 9.45 am and finished at the time given,
work out how many minutes they were swimming.

   a Gerry: 10.05 am   **b** Hannah: 10.07 am
   c Zak: 10.01 am   **d** Polly: 10.26 am
   e Maggie: 10.21 am   **f** Tariq: 10.13 am

CHALLENGE

Draw other arrow diagrams
like this using the swimmers in **5** .

Hannah ⟶ swam 120 m further than ⟶ Gerry
Hannah ⟶ swam 180 m further than ⟶ Zak

Stamp division

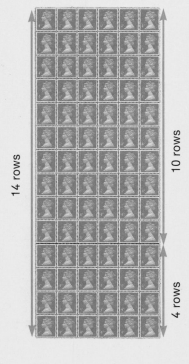

14 rows

10 rows

4 rows

- If there are 84 stamps in rows of 6, estimate how many rows there will be.

- Find out if your estimate is correct.

This is one way to work out the answer as a division → using the x10 and x4 tables.

$$
\begin{array}{r}
14 \\
6{\overline{\smash{)}84}} \\
-60 \text{ (10 rows of 6)} \\
\hline
24 \text{ stamps left} \\
-24 \text{ (4 rows of 6)} \\
\hline
0 \text{ stamps left}
\end{array}
$$

14 rows of 6 stamps

1 Use the stamps to help you. Copy and complete the divisions.

a

$$
\begin{array}{r}
\Box\Box \\
3{\overline{\smash{)}42}} \\
-\Box\Box \text{ (10 rows of 3)} \\
\hline
12 \text{ stamps left} \\
-\Box\Box \text{ (4 rows of 3)} \\
\hline
0 \text{ stamps left}
\end{array}
$$

$\Box\Box$ rows of stamps

b
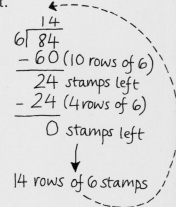

$$
\begin{array}{r}
\Box\Box \\
9{\overline{\smash{)}108}} \\
-\Box\Box \text{ (10 rows of } \Box\text{)} \\
\hline
18 \text{ stamps left} \\
-\Box\Box \text{ (2 rows of } \Box\text{)} \\
\hline
0 \text{ stamps left}
\end{array}
$$

$\Box\Box$ rows of stamps

2 Work out how many rows in these blocks of stamps.

a 56 stamps in rows of 4.   **b** 75 stamps in rows of 5.
c 51 stamps in rows of 3.   **d** 72 stamps in rows of 6.
e 84 stamps in rows of 7.   **f** 135 stamps in rows of 9.

Paper folding

1 Fold the shapes into quarters each time.

 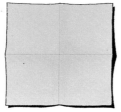 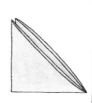  

2 Find ways to make these patterns by cutting.
Stick them in your book.
Mark the axes of symmetry with a felt-tip pen.

*Each shape has **2** axes of symmetry.*

a 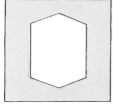 b  c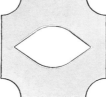

d  e  f  g

3 Make 3 more patterns of your own.
Stick them in your book.
Mark the axes of symmetry.

CHALLENGE

- Investigate ways to make patterns with paper shapes like these folded into quarters.

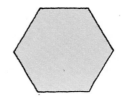 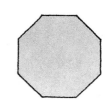

Two lines of symmetry

1 cm squared paper or RM A, mirror

This pattern has 2 lines of symmetry.
Check by placing your mirror on
the dotted lines.

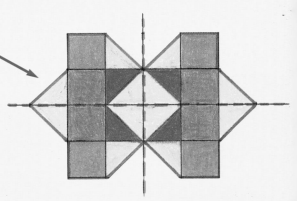

1   Copy and complete these patterns.
    You can use a mirror to help.

> Each pattern has
> 2 lines of symmetry.

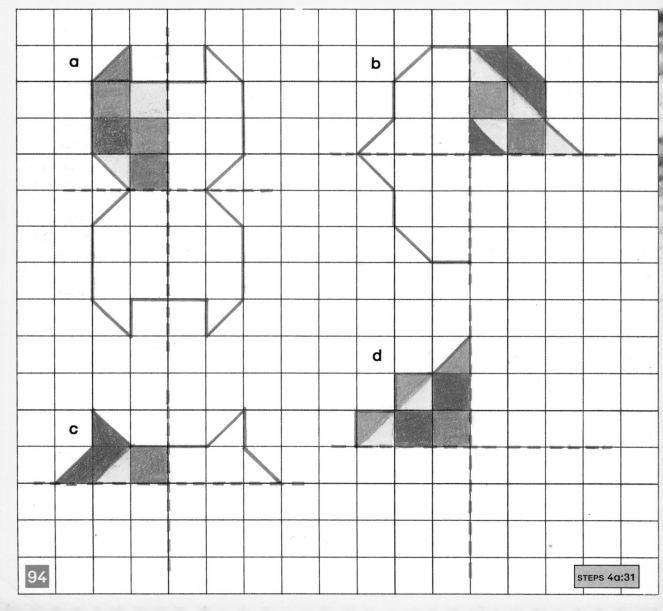

a

b

c

d

94

Symmetry puzzles

mirror, 1 cm squared paper or RM A

1 This shape has **2 axes of symmetry**.

a Draw more shapes using 9 squares that have 2 axes of symmetry.

b Try again, this time using 12 squares. Record your findings.

> *Mark the axes of symmetry on your drawings.*

2 **a** Cut out 2 shapes like this:

b Fit the 2 shapes together in different ways to make larger shapes with 2 axes of symmetry.

c Try again, this time using 2 matching shapes made from 8 squares.

> Use a mirror to check.

3 Place a mirror on this triangle so that you can see:

a a large square

b a kite

c an isosceles triangle.

4 **a** Investigate other shapes you can make by placing a mirror on the triangle.

b Draw some of the interesting ones. Can your friend decide where you placed the mirror to make these shapes?

CHALLENGE

- Use the shape in **1**.

- Investigate ways to place a mirror so that you can see 1 square, 2 squares ... 18 squares.

Colin sorted shapes on this Venn diagram.

We put block **a** in region **3** because it **is** blue, **is** circular, but **is not** a large block.

blue 2 3 4 circular
1 5 6 7
8 large

1 Write the number of the region **you** think each shape should go in.

Use logic blocks and a sorting diagram if it helps you.

a

b

c

d

e

f

g

i

h

k

j

l

m

n

o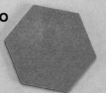

STEPS 4a:32

■ Button sort ■ ■ ■ ■ ■ ■ ■ ■

Sandra and Sally sorted out buttons on to this Venn diagram.

We put button **a** in region 7 because it **is** red and **has** two holes and **is less than 2 cm** in diameter.

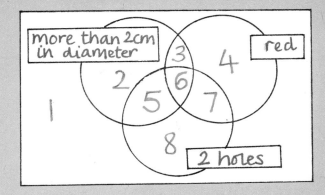

more than 2 cm in diameter

red

2 holes

1

1 | Write the number of the region you think each button should go in.

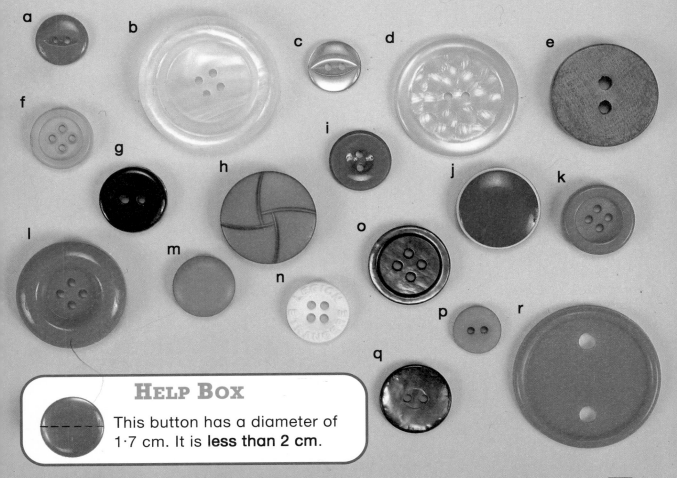

HELP BOX

This button has a diameter of 1·7 cm. It is **less than 2 cm**.

This decision tree has been used to sort some **triangles**, **quadrilaterals**, **pentagons** and **hexagons**.

REMEMBER
A **regular shape** has all its sides and angles equal.

You could work with a friend to answer the questions on the next page.

START HERE

Has it any right-angles?

YES — Is it regular?
YES — Is it green?
YES → A
NO → B

NO — Is it green?
YES → C
NO → D

NO — Is it regular?
YES — Is it green?
YES → E
NO → F

NO — Is it green?
YES → G
NO → H

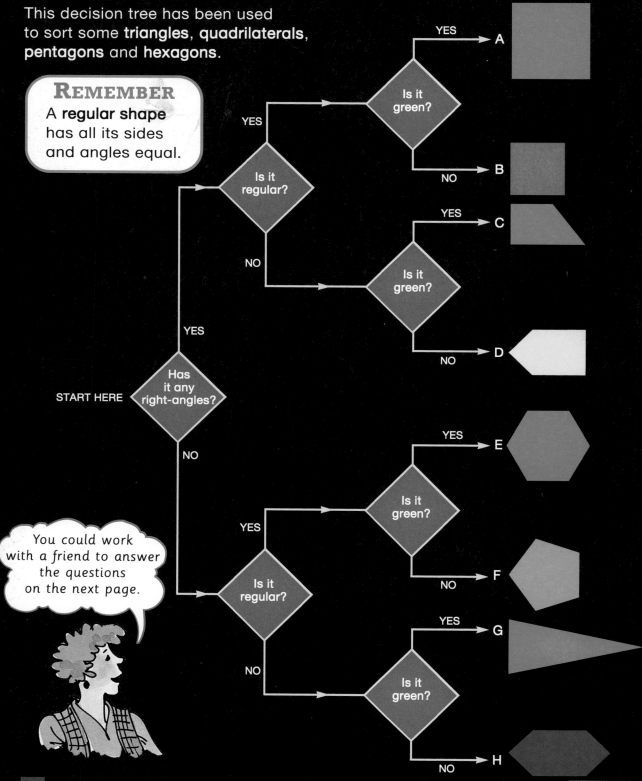

1 Draw and colour the shapes described here.

Use the decision tree to help you answer 1 , 2 , and 3 .

  a It has right angles. It is regular. It is green.
  b It has no right angles. It is regular. It is green.
  c It has right angles. It is not regular. It is not green.
  d It has no right angles. It is not regular. It is green.

2 Write about these shapes in the same way.

a   **b**   **c**  **d**

3 The end of the branches are lettered A, B, C, D, E, F, G and H.
Write where these shapes will end up.

a   **b**  **c**   **d** 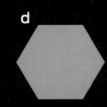 **e**

CHALLENGE

- Use these questions to design a decision tree with **8** end branches.

  Is it an even number?
  Is it > 10?
  Is it a multiple of 3?

- Sort each number from 1 to 20 on to the end branches.

Sorting them out

A group of children were talking in the cloakroom about their heights, weights and shoe sizes.

I weigh 42 kg.
I take size 3 shoes.
I'm 138 cm tall.

I'm 143 cm tall.
I weigh 38 kg.
My shoes are size 3.

Ann

Chi

I take size 6 shoes.
I'm 145 cm tall.
I weigh 37 kg.

I only take size 2s.
I'm 141 cm tall and
I weigh 43 kg.

Fran

Em

Hugh

Bill

I weigh 41 kg
and I'm 145 cm tall.
My shoes are size 4.

My shoes are the same size as Chi's
but I'm 135 cm tall and
I weigh 37 kg.

I take size 5s and
weigh 44 kg.
I'm 139 cm tall.

I'm 130 cm tall,
weigh 38 kg and
take size 4 shoes.

Gail

Dan

1 Use these measurements to help you complete RM 125.

Tessellating triangles

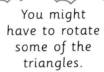

Here is a tessellation of triangles, partly coloured.

1   Decide how to test matching triangles
like these to see if they tessellate.

Choose materials to help you.

> You might
> have to rotate
> some of the
> triangles.

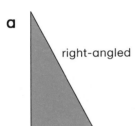

a   right-angled

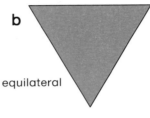

b   equilateral

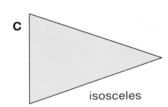

c   isosceles

d   scalene

This is what Jim thinks:

> Matching triangles
> can always tessellate.

2   Write what **you** think.

CHALLENGE

Try to find a way to make this tessellate.

non-regular quadrilateral

Regular polygons

You can make tessellations with one regular shape ...

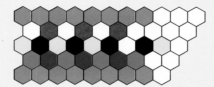

... or with more than one. This is a **semi-regular tessellation**.

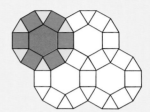

1   Name the three shapes used in the semi-regular tessellation above.

2   Decide the best way to construct and draw tessellations like these.

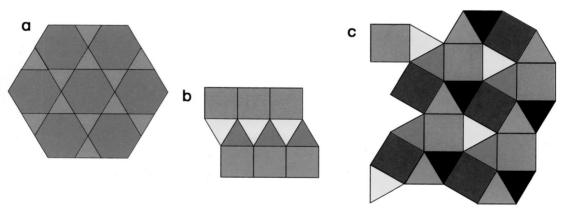

a   b   c

3   Try to make other semi-regular tessellations using these shapes.

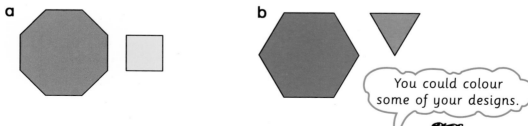

a   b

You could colour some of your designs.

CHALLENGE

Try to draw the semi-regular tessellation shown at the top of the page.

Your own tessellation

rectangles of card, sticky tape, scissors, large sheets of paper

1   Make your own tessellation.

- Cut a rectangle of card into two pieces from one corner to another, like this.

- Translate the cut-out piece to the opposite side.

- Flip over the cut-out piece and tape it in place.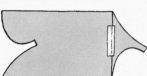

- Cut another piece from one side, like this.

- Translate the cut-out piece to the opposite side and tape it in place.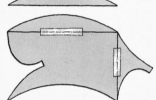

2   Draw round your shape and try to make it tessellate.
Look carefully to see how the tile on this page tessellates.

If you don't like your tile, try again.

Decorate all or part of your design.

CHALLENGE
What happens if you flip **both** pieces?

■ Scale ■ ■ ■ ■ ■ ■ ■ ■ ■

These pencils are shown **half-scale**.
This is sometimes called a **scale of 1 to 2**.
They are really **twice as big** as shown here.

Scale		
———	**represents**	———
1 cm		2 cm

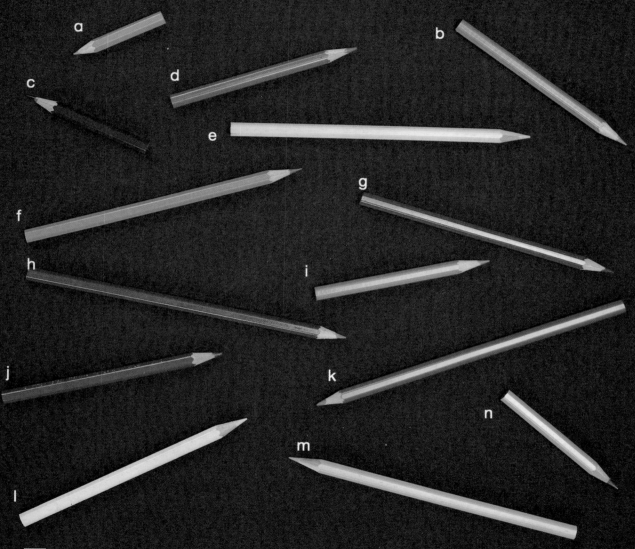

1   Measure the length of each pencil
    in millimetres.

2   Copy and complete this table
    for each pencil. ⟶

pencil	half-scale length (mm)	real length (mm)	real length (cm)
a			

Here are three pencils shown **actual size**.
This is sometimes called a **1 to 1 scale**.

	Scale	
___	**represents**	___
1 cm		1 cm

a

b

c

> Think about the length **and** the width.

3   Decide the best way to draw them half-scale.

Sometimes objects are drawn bigger
than they really are so that you can
see the small details.

	Scale	
___	**represents**	___
2 cm		1 cm

Here are some caterpillars shown double their size.
This is sometimes called a **2 to 1 scale**.

4   Copy and complete this table for each one. ⟶

caterpillar	double-scale length (mm)	real length (mm)	real length (cm)
a			

a

Swallowtail Butterfly

b

Cinnabar Moth

c

Small Copper Butterfly

d

Wood White Butterfly

e

Feathered Thorn Moth

CHALLENGE

Find some objects > 5 cm long. Draw them using a scale of **2 to 1**.

Doubling and halving

This rectangle is 4 cm long
and 3 cm wide.
Its area is 12 square centimetres.

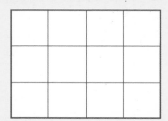

3 cm

1   Draw a rectangle of this length and width
on centimetre squared paper. Write its area underneath.

2   Double the length of each side and draw the larger rectangle.
Write its area underneath.

3   Repeat stages 1 and 2 for these rectangles.

a   2 cm   4 cm

b   3 cm   3 cm

c   5 cm   3 cm

d   7 cm   1 cm

e   6 cm   3 cm

4   Do the same for rectangles of these lengths and widths.

a   4 cm long, 4 cm wide   b   6 cm long, 2 cm wide
c   8 cm long, 1 cm wide   d   5 cm long, 4 cm wide

5   Look at your results, then complete this sentence to show what you think.
When you double the sides of a rectangle, the area ...

CHALLENGE

David doubled the sides of a rectangle so that its area became 96 sq cm.
Draw the 4 different rectangles David might have started with.

STEPS 4a:34

6 Copy and complete each rectangle so that it has the given area. Write its area underneath.
Next to each one, draw a rectangle whose sides are **half as long**. Write its area underneath.

1 cm squared
paper or RM A

d

a

b

c

72 sq cm

e

48 sq cm

48 sq cm

96 sq cm

f

80 sq cm

56 sq cm

7 Write about how the area has changed in the smaller rectangles.

CHALLENGE

If you double the length of the sides of these shapes,
each will have an area of 20 sq cm.
Draw the shapes to show
this is true.

Doubling letters

If you double the length of the sides of this letter L ...

Area = 3 sq cm

... it is enlarged like this:

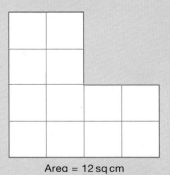

Area = 12 sq cm

1 Copy each of these letters on to squared paper.
Alongside each one, draw it enlarged so that the length
of each side is doubled.

a   b   c   d

e   f

2 Underneath each letter, write its area
in square centimetres.

3 Complete this sentence.
**When you double the length of the sides
of a shape, the area ...**

f is much harder!

CHALLENGE

Choose materials to help you draw
the letters in ☐1☐ to **half-scale**.

Estimating capacities

½ litre calibrated jug, Plasticine, yoghurt pots

1 Use a jug, water and Plasticine.

  a Start with **300 ml** of water in the jug.

  b Make a ball of Plasticine which you estimate will make the water level rise to **350 ml** when you put it in the jug.

  c Check your estimate.

  d Add or remove Plasticine until you get it right.

  e Make another ball of Plasticine in the same way to make the water level rise to 500 ml.

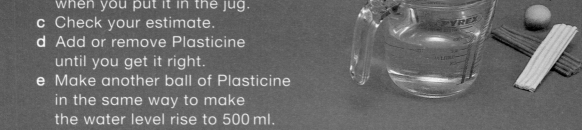

2 Use 3 identical yoghurt pots.

  a Fill one of the pots with water.

  b Share the amount in the full pot so that all three pots contain the same amount.

  c Write how you did it.

3 Write **true** or **false** for each of these statements.

  a 250 ml < ¼ of a litre   **b** 1½ litres = 1400 ml

  c $\frac{1}{10}$ of a litre = 100 ml   **d** 800 ml > ¾ of a litre

  e 50% of a litre < 500 ml   **f** A milk bottle holds less than 100 ml.

4 Write the **best estimate** of the capacity of these things.

a teaspoon	20 ml	10 ml	5 ml
b tea cup	50 ml	200 ml	600 ml
c thimble	10 ml	5 ml	2 ml
d yoghurt pot	10 ml	50 ml	150 ml
e egg cup	5 ml	50 ml	100 ml
f bath	1 litre	100 ml	1000 litres

Calculating capacities

1   How many cupfuls will fill these containers?

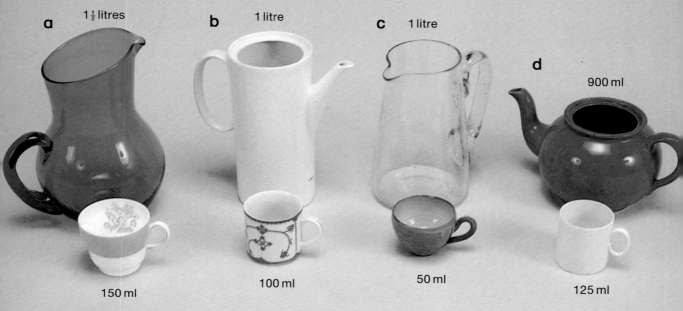

a $1\frac{1}{2}$ litres

b 1 litre

c 1 litre

d 900 ml

150 ml

100 ml

50 ml

125 ml

2   Use the bar-line graph to answer the questions.

  a Which container has the greatest capacity?
  b Which containers hold more than 600 ml?
  c What is the total capacity of the mug
     and cup together?
  d What is the difference between
     the capacities of the bowl and the jug?
  e If a glass of water was poured from the bottle,
     how much would be left?
  f Could you pour 3 mugfuls from the bottle?

3   A bottle of squash holds 1 litre.
   A drink is made using **50 ml** of squash and **200 ml** of water.

  a How many drinks could be made from the one-litre bottle?
  b How much water would be used to make the drinks?

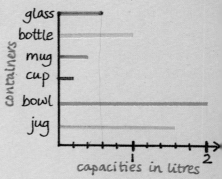

> ## CHALLENGE
> How many bottles of squash would you need to make
> a drink for everyone in your class? Your school?

Comparing fractions

REMEMBER

> means 'is larger than'
< means 'is smaller than'

Ordering fractions

1 Copy. Write > or < between each pair.

a $\frac{1}{2}$ $\frac{2}{5}$ b $\frac{3}{4}$ $\frac{4}{5}$ c $\frac{5}{6}$ $\frac{3}{4}$

d $\frac{7}{10}$ $\frac{3}{4}$ e $\frac{3}{5}$ $\frac{5}{8}$ f $\frac{2}{3}$ $\frac{5}{8}$

2 Write 3 more statements like these in your book.

one whole									
$\frac{1}{2}$					$\frac{1}{2}$				
$\frac{1}{3}$			$\frac{1}{3}$			$\frac{1}{3}$			
$\frac{1}{4}$		$\frac{1}{4}$		$\frac{1}{4}$			$\frac{1}{4}$		
$\frac{1}{5}$		$\frac{1}{5}$	$\frac{1}{5}$		$\frac{1}{5}$		$\frac{1}{5}$		
$\frac{1}{6}$	$\frac{1}{6}$	$\frac{1}{6}$	$\frac{1}{6}$		$\frac{1}{6}$		$\frac{1}{6}$		
$\frac{1}{8}$	$\frac{1}{8}$	$\frac{1}{8}$	$\frac{1}{8}$	$\frac{1}{8}$	$\frac{1}{8}$	$\frac{1}{8}$	$\frac{1}{8}$		
$\frac{1}{10}$	$\frac{1}{10}$	$\frac{1}{10}$	$\frac{1}{10}$	$\frac{1}{10}$	$\frac{1}{10}$	$\frac{1}{10}$	$\frac{1}{10}$	$\frac{1}{10}$	$\frac{1}{10}$

Matching fractions

The same amount is coloured on these 2 rectangles.
So $\frac{1}{4}$ and $\frac{2}{8}$ are **equivalent fractions**.
So we can write $\dfrac{1}{4} = \dfrac{2}{8}$.

3 Write the **equivalent fractions** coloured on these shapes.

a   b 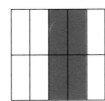   c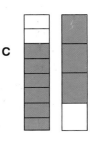

4

a $\frac{4}{6} = \frac{\blacksquare}{3}$ b $\frac{3}{4} = \frac{\square}{8}$ c $\frac{8}{10} = \frac{4}{\blacksquare}$ d $\frac{1}{2} = \frac{\blacksquare}{6}$ e $\frac{1}{2} = \frac{\blacksquare}{10}$ f $\frac{2}{8} = \frac{\blacksquare}{4}$

CHALLENGE

Choose a suitable shape from one of these to show each of the fractions below.

• Draw round the shape. • Rule lines on your drawing. • Colour in the fraction.

a $\frac{3}{4}$ b $\frac{5}{6}$ c $\frac{2}{3}$ d $\frac{7}{10}$ e $\frac{4}{5}$ f $\frac{5}{8}$ g $\frac{7}{12}$

Colouring fractions

1 cm squared
paper or RM A

1 Draw 6 grids like **A** on squared paper.

   a Divide one grid into **fifths**.
      Colour each fifth a different colour.

   b Find **five** other ways
      of dividing the grid into fifths.

A

2 Draw grids like **B** on squared paper.

   a Investigate ways to colour
      quarters on one grid.

   b Investigate ways to colour
      other fractions on the other grids.
      Use different colours
      and label the fractions.

B

*You can find
halves, thirds ...*

CHALLENGE

How many **different** fractions can you show
by colouring whole squares on grids like this?

There are more than 10!

Fraction problems

counters, 1 cm squared paper or RM A

This is $\frac{1}{5}$ of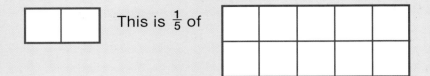

1 Use squared paper and draw 4 more whole shapes in which  is:

a $\frac{1}{5}$ **b** $\frac{1}{2}$ **c** $\frac{1}{3}$ **d** $\frac{1}{6}$ **e** $\frac{1}{4}$.

2 Draw 12 buttons.
Colour $\frac{1}{3}$ yellow and the rest red.

   a How many buttons are yellow?   **b** How many buttons are red?

   c What fraction is red?   **d** What is $\frac{1}{3}$ of 12?   **e** What is $\frac{2}{3}$ of 12?

3 Draw two circles.

   a Choose a number of counters.
Try to put $\frac{1}{3}$ in the first circle.

Try to put $\frac{2}{3}$ in the second circle.

   b Try different numbers of counters.

   c Write what you find on a chart like this.

   d Afterwards, write what you notice about each column of numbers.

first circle $\frac{1}{3}$	second circle $\frac{2}{3}$	total number of counters
2	4	6

4 In a class of 28 children $\frac{1}{4}$ were aged 9. The rest were aged 10.

   a How many children were aged 9?   **b** What fraction was aged 10?

   c What is $\frac{1}{4}$ of 28?   **d** What is $\frac{3}{4}$ of 28?

CHALLENGE

- Investigate the different numbers of counters you could have in two circles, if you put $\frac{2}{5}$ in the first circle and $\frac{3}{5}$ in the second circle.

- Write your results in a chart.

Fractions and division

To find $\frac{1}{3}$ of a set, we divide the number into 3 equal parts.

$$\frac{1}{3} \text{ of } 9 = 3 \qquad 9 \div 3 = 3$$

1 Write the answers only.

    a $15 \div 3$ **b** $\frac{1}{3}$ of 15   **c** $24 \div 3$ **d** $\frac{1}{3}$ of 24

    e $18 \div 3$ **f** $\frac{1}{3}$ of 18   **g** $30 \div 3$ **h** $\frac{1}{3}$ of 30

2 Copy and complete these.

    a ⬡ $\div 5 = 3$ **b** $\frac{1}{5}$ of ⬡ $= 3$ **c** ⬡ $\div 5 = 6$ **d** $\frac{1}{5}$ of ⬡ $= 6$

    e $\frac{1}{5}$ of ⬡ $= 5$ **f** $\frac{1}{5}$ of ⬡ $= 10$ **g** $\frac{1}{5}$ of ⬡ $= 2$ **h** $\frac{1}{5}$ of ⬡ $= 20$

3 Now try these.

    a $\frac{1}{4}$ of $24 = 6$ **b** $\frac{1}{3}$ of $27 = 9$ **c** $\frac{1}{2}$ of $50 = 25$ **d** $\frac{1}{5}$ of $40 = 8$

    e $\frac{1}{6}$ of $24 = 4$ **f** $\frac{1}{8}$ of $8 = 1$ **g** $\frac{1}{10}$ of $90 = 9$ **h** $\frac{1}{7}$ of $14 = 2$

4 How many minutes in:

    a 1 hour   **b** $\frac{1}{2}$ hour   **c** $\frac{1}{4}$ hour   **d** $\frac{3}{4}$ hour

    e $\frac{1}{3}$ hour   **f** $\frac{1}{5}$ hour   **g** $\frac{1}{6}$ hour   **h** $\frac{1}{10}$ hour?

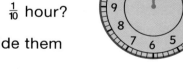

5   **a** Draw more lines like this one and divide them into equal parts.

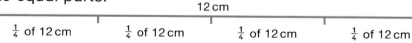

12 cm

$\frac{1}{4}$ of 12 cm $\frac{1}{4}$ of 12 cm $\frac{1}{4}$ of 12 cm $\frac{1}{4}$ of 12 cm

Try to show all fractions from $\frac{1}{2}$ to $\frac{1}{10}$ on your lines.

CHALLENGE

Jessica had 24 sweets and ate $\frac{1}{4}$ of them.

She gave $\frac{1}{3}$ of those left to Gopal.

Then she gave $\frac{1}{4}$ of those still left to Penny.

How many sweets does Jessica still have?

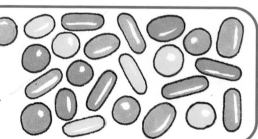

Reading a graph ■ ■ ■ ■ ■

Alice and Peter designed this line graph to show the outdoor temperatures they had recorded.

1 At what times did they start and finish?

2 Use the plotted points to find the time when the temperature was:

    a 11°C   **b** 7°C   **c** 10°C.

3 Write the temperature when it was:

    a coolest in the morning
    b coolest in the afternoon.

4 Write the temperatures at these times:

    a 1 pm   **b** 9 am   **c** 11 am.

5 Between which two times did this happen.

    a The temperature rose 2°C.
    b The temperature rose 5°C.
    c The temperature dropped 2°C.
    d The temperature dropped 5°C.
    e The temperature rose 7°C.

6 Estimate the likely temperature at:

    a   **b**

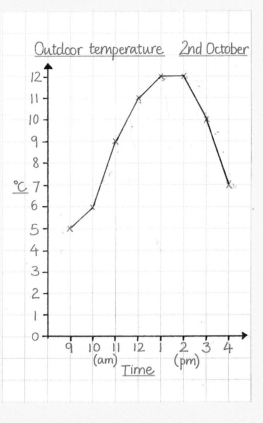

Outdoor temperature 2nd October

Shadow graph

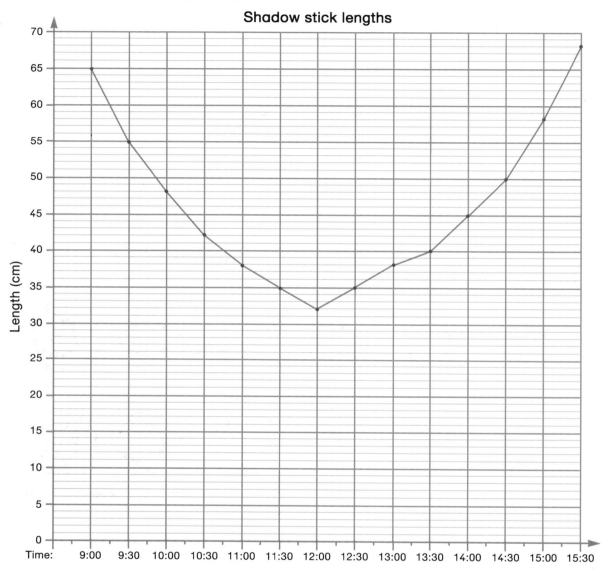

Shadow stick lengths

Length (cm)

Time: 9:00 9:30 10:00 10:30 11:00 11:30 12:00 12:30 13:00 13:30 14:00 14:30 15:00 15:30

Laura and Zoe measured the length of a stick's shadow throughout the day.

116

1 Write how many times Laura and Zoe measured the shadow.

2 Write the length of the shadow at these times:

a `09:30` b `10:00` c `12:00` d `15:30`

3 Write the time when the shadow was this length.

a 38 cm **b** 40 cm **c** 58 cm **d** at its longest **e** at its shortest

4 Write two times when the shadow was 35 cm long.

5 Write two more times when the shadows were the same length.

6 How much shorter did the shadow become between these times?

a `09:00` and `09:30` b `11:30` and `12:00` c `09:00` and `12:00`

7 How much longer did the shadow become between these times?

a `15:00` and `15:30` b `12:00` and `12:30` c `12:00` and `15:30`

8 If it is sunny from 7:00 until 19:00, estimate the length of the shadow at:

a `08:00` b `16:30` c `17:00` d `20:00`

> **CHALLENGE**
> Work out the approximate length of the shadow
> at 09:15 and every half-hour until 15:15.

STEPS 4a:37

117

Drawing a graph ■ ■ ■ ■

1 cm squared
paper or RM A

These parts of 8 thermometers show the outdoor temperatures recorded every
hour on 13 January.

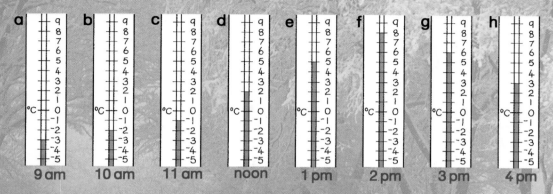

| a | b | c | d | e | f | g | h |
| 9 am | 10 am | 11 am | noon | 1 pm | 2 pm | 3 pm | 4 pm |

1 Copy and complete this table.

Time	9 am	10 am						
Temperature (°C)								

2 Draw a line graph to show this information. Glue it in your book
if it is on loose paper. You might use the graph on page 115 to help you.

3 **a** Write 5 questions you could ask someone about your graph.
  b Under each question, write the answer.

CHALLENGE

Here are the temperatures taken hourly
from 9.00 am to 4.00 pm on a hot summer's day.

Design a line graph using these clues.

- The temperature was the same at 10 am and 4 pm.
- It was 2°C cooler at 11 am than at noon.
- It was 5°C hotter at 2 pm than at 4 pm.
- It was 26°C at noon but 4°C hotter an hour later.
- At 4 pm, the temperature was 4°C cooler than at noon
  but 5°C hotter than at 9 am.
- It was 3°C cooler at 10 am than at 3 pm.

22°C   17°C   24°C   25°C   26°C   27°C   30°C   22°C

Writing locations

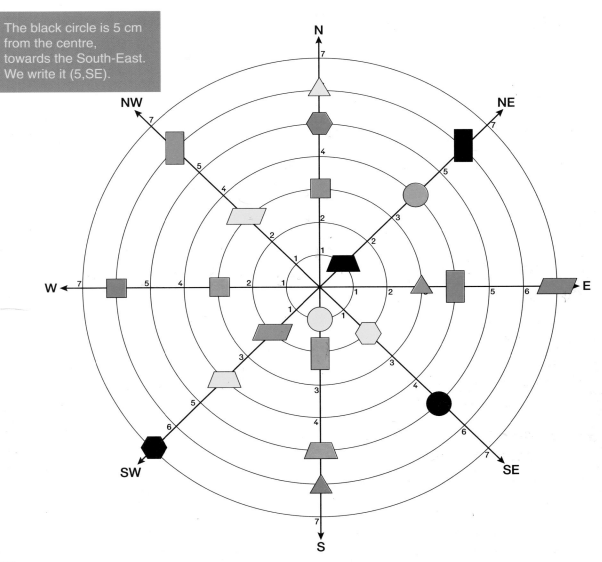

The black circle is 5 cm from the centre, towards the South-East. We write it (5,SE).

1 Write the position of these coloured shapes in the same way as in the red box.

    a red square   **b** yellow hexagon   **c** green triangle   **d** black circle
    e blue oblong   **f** red parallelogram   **g** yellow trapezium   **h** green square
    i blue circle   **j** green hexagon   **k** blue trapezium   **l** red oblong

2 Write the colour and name of the shapes at these points.

    a (6,NE)   **b** (3,W)   **c** (3,NW)   **d** (7,E)   **e** (1,NE)
    f (1,S)   **g** (7,SW)   **h** (6,N)   **i** (4,E)   **j** (3,E)

Cracking the code

■ ■ ■ ■ ■

1   Use the grid to work out this message.

(3,W)

(5,S) (3,W) (2,N) (5,W)

(3,SE) (2,NW) (3,W) (1,E) (2,S)

(4,SE) (4,NW) (1,NW) (4,SW) (5,E)

> ### REMEMBER
>
> Write the distance from the centre, **then** the direction. A is at (4,NW).

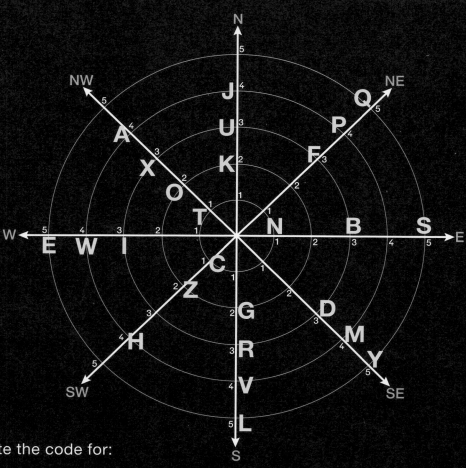

2   Write the code for:

a   your name   **b**   a friend's name

c   your teacher's name   **d**   your favourite game or sport.

> ### CHALLENGE
> - Work with a friend.
> - Make up messages in code using the grid above.
> - Swap them and decode the messages.

Map directions

Scale 1 cm on the map represents 1 km on the ground.

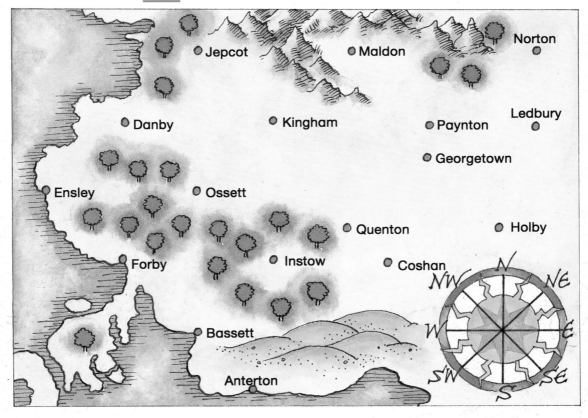

1 Which town is about:

   a 4 km South of Ossett   b 5 km North-West of Anterton
   c 3 km North-East of Ensley   d 7 km South-West of Norton
   e 4 km West of Holby   f 11 km East of Danby
   g 3 km South-East of Jepcot   h 8 km North of Bassett?

2 Make up five more questions about the distances
   and directions on the map.

CHALLENGE

• Use a map of Great Britain.
• Find the town you live in or the one nearest to you.
• Find towns to the North, South, East and West of it.
• Find the distance they are from the place where you live.

Drawing shapes

These instructions tell you how to draw this shape.

Start at 0.
Cross 3 squares NE
then 3 squares S
then 3 squares W.

0

N
NW   NE
W   E
SW   SE
S

1   Use squared paper. Follow the instructions to draw the shapes.

a
Start at 0.
Cross 4 squares SE
then 3 squares W
then cross 4 squares NW
then 3 squares E.

b
Start at 0.
Cross 3 squares NE
then 2 squares E
then cross 3 squares SE
then 8 squares W.

c
Start at 0.
Cross 3 squares SW
then 3 squares NW
then cross 3 squares NE
then 3 squares SE.

2   Write the instructions for the 'return journey' for each shape.

3   Write the instructions for each of these shapes: • going clockwise
                                                          • going anticlockwise.

a

0

b

0

c

0

4   Draw a shape of your own on squared paper.
        Write the instructions for how you drew it.